SAM SNEAD'S BOOK OF GOLF
Keys to Lifelong Success

J McQueen

SAM SNEAD'S BOOK OF GOLF

Keys to Lifelong Success

by Sam Snead with Larry Sheehan

Technical Editor Ken Bowden
Illustrated by Jim McQueen

Stanley Paul, London

Stanley Paul & Co. Ltd
3 Fitzroy Square, London w 1 p 6jd

An imprint of the Hutchinson Publishing Group

London Melbourne Sydney Auckland
Wellington Johannesburg and agencies
throughout the world

First published in Great Britain 1975
This edition 1979
© Sam Snead and Larry Sheehan 1975

Printed by The Anchor Press Ltd and bound by
Wm Brendon & Son Ltd, both of
Tiptree, Essex

ISBN 0 09 125311 X

Introduction

A FEW years ago I asked twenty-five of the America's top tournament professionals who they thought had the best golf swing on tour for an article in *Golf Digest* magazine. Most chose Sam Snead, and many of those who did not select him as number one named him among their top three.

More recently the inductees into Pinehurst's Golf Hall of Fame voted among themselves to name the greatest golfer of all time. They chose Sam Snead.

It's a safe bet—at least for my money— that if you asked weekend golfers around the world to pick the greatest golf swing in history, the majority would choose Sam Snead's.

There are some good reasons for all this approbation. First, Samuel Jackson Snead has played his game longer and better than any sportsman of record, which is a tribute to his technique as much as to his athleticism and desire. Second, throughout his forty-plus years of almost daily competition, Snead has almost never slumped—has been a prime contender almost every time he teed up—which, to my mind, is an even greater testimonial to his technique than his actual record, fantastic as that is. Third, and in my view the factor most responsible for his universal appeal, is his grace. With the possible exception of Harry Vardon—and excepting his endeavors on the putting greens—Snead has made golf look easier and more beautiful than any professional player in history.

There can be little doubt that this grace—the indelible ease and beauty of his swing—is as much the product of luck as of conscious will and effort. Snead's magnificent physique and superb reflexes are gifts of nature that few are given. Yet the fact that the rest of us fall short of his inherent talent does not disqualify him as a model. Indeed, the value of Snead's swing as an example for all is proven daily on the tour by the size of his galleries. Only the current superstars and the tournament leaders (and not always the latter) regularly attract more followers among active golfers. The reason is simple if often subconscious: watching Snead, it is impossible not to feel that your own swing will instantly improve. Just a few holes in his gallery and the game begins to look so ridiculously easy that you feel you must vastly improve at it if you were to go out and play immediately.

I believe this book will have the same effect on most readers, but with much more substantial and lasting benefits. There are three reasons why so.

First and foremost, what Snead does with a golf club may not be precisely copyable by the average mortal, but in *overall style and form and essence* it most certainly is. And the reason why his swing is so copyable is the same reason that has enabled him to remain a serious contender well into his sixties: minimization of physical contortion and muscular strain. The golf swing always has been and always will be a physically complex and contortive action, and in my view the ever-increasing emphasis in modern teaching on the ever-more-mechanistic techniques of the professional tour exacerbate those problems for the purely recreational golfer.

Snead is the ultimate antidote to this poison. His swing is certainly "mechanical" in the sense that it repeats—is, as he often says in these pages, "grooved." Yet it is also the most natural of swings in that it demands the minimum amount of bodily contortion or muscular strain. That, along with its marvelously smooth tempo, is why it is so beautiful—and also why it is such a superb model for Mr. and Ms. Average.

The second factor about this book that will lead a great many people to better and more enjoyable golf is its basic simplicity and straightforwardness. One reason Snead's previous books about technique left something to be desired was his difficulty—especially during his hectic peak playing years—in intellectually orchestrating and then verbally communicating precisely how he played a game that he had learned virtually unaided and almost totally by "feel," through trial and error. Now, with age forcing him more and more to analyze his technique in order to preserve it, and with more time available, and with the help of a skilled and committed professional writer, he has been able to cover the subject totally and definitively. But in Snead's case that does not mean complicatedly. His approach to the golf swing has always been as simple, direct, and down-home as he could possibly make it; he has avoided superfluity of intellectualization as rigorously as he has shunned superfluity of physical action. This book does exactly the same, while covering not only the "how" but the "why" of every truly important facet of playing technique.

The third factor through which this book, carefully absorbed, will bring much help to struggling hackers and strong but erratic players alike is the golfing attitude of mind it reveals. A cautious, private, highly-independent fellow by birth and background, Snead has rarely seen fit to reveal even to close acquaintances what goes on inside his head when he plays golf, let alone to the world at large. Those parts of the book in which he uninhibitedly does so will be as invaluable to the mentally discombobulated player as the swing keys will be to the golfer whose technique has been mixed up.

Ken Bowden, 1975

Contents

CONTENTS

PART III THE SWING IN ACTION

PART IV COMPETING

Part I
PHILOSOPHY

1 : You Have More Potential Than You Think You Have

WHAT'S the practical challenge in golf?

To get off the tee straight.

To keep up your concentration for the second shot.

To learn to play all the around-the-green shots as well as you can.

To get the ball in the cup on each green in no more than two strokes.

That about covers the game, don't you think? Anybody who can do that for eighteen holes is bound to shoot in the 80s or better.

Yet more than half the people playing golf around the world today can't break 100!

And that's in spite of all kinds of advances in such things as golf equipment and golf-course care.

When I started playing golf, there was no such thing as the pitching wedge or sand iron, the two great scoring weapons from a hundred yards in today. And yardage-producing metal shafts were only just coming along—my first "modern" driver had little holes drilled through the shaft, and it whistled a tune every time I swung.

PART I PHILOSOPHY

Golf-course maintenance is a whole lot better overall, nowadays, but its main contribution to scoring has come on the greens. Turf know-how and fancy grooming tools have turned putting into a far less chancy proposition than it used to be. Weeds and worm casts and such are things of the past, and today's greens putt pretty much the way they look—true.

There have also been advances in instruction. Or, at least, a lot more attention has been given to refining and codifying and communicating the "how" and "why" of golf than was given in earlier decades. Today's teaching professionals probably have more knowledge and dedication than ever before. And they're getting the game's fundamentals across to those new golfers who will listen in fast, effective ways.

And what about the golfers themselves? People today are bigger and stronger than ever before. They're in better health and in better physical shape for performing any sport, golf included.

Yet, as I've mentioned, in spite of all this progress, *most average golfers today can't break 100 for a round.* That fact was confirmed for me not long ago in a *Golf Digest* study of some half million handicap cards from all across the country. It aroused my worst suspicions about the state of the popular—as opposed to the pro—game today, and made me wonder how many people might be staying away from golf, or giving it up, because they find it too hard to score well, or more trouble than it's worth, or just plain no fun to play.

Something's wrong somewhere. Hard as this game is—and I'd be the first to call golf the most complex mixture of do's and don'ts in sport—there should be some way for more people to play it more enjoyably, which of course means better. I don't mean pro-tour better. I just mean better in relation to a person's natural potential.

I've spent a lot of time with all kinds of pupils on the lesson tee in between tournaments over the years. From what I've seen, I'm inclined to believe most people *do* have more potential for improvement than they think they have. Most people, if they use their abilities properly and hold onto their common sense, can get around the meanest track with a decent-looking score.

That's more or less the spirit in which this book is presented. If I have a particular aim here, it is to help make it as easy as possible for a person to play golf as well as possible—and for as long as possible. Remember, one of the great things about golf is that it is a lifetime proposition. The length of my own playing career shows that the kind of golf swing I'm talking about getting more people to use *does* stand up over the years.

I hope in this book to clear the air about a lot that's been said and done on how to play golf. I learned to play from the ground up, so to speak, all by myself. I'm not reporting that out of pride, especially. If I'd been able to take golf lessons as a kid, I probably would have jumped at the chance. It just happened I didn't. And by having to slowly and stubbornly teach myself, I believe I got a hold on the game according to what really counts, and in a way that applies to most folks.

As a result, my views may sound too simple and straightforward at times, but I've never been a great believer in complicating an issue unnecessarily. A lot of instructional talk today comes out of the rare air in which a couple of hundred unusually gifted and highly trained touring pros operate, and really contributes little or nothing useful to the game of the weekend golfer.

I happen to feel that if you're only responsible for giving first aid, it's a mistake to study up on the techniques of open-heart surgery—which is the error many ordinary golfers make when they try to apply fragments of a champion professional's knowledge to their own games. Anyway, in this book we'll be following the premise that a lot of things really *are* simpler than they're made out to be.

I don't deny that *learning* the game can be tricky, however. I once improved a man's grip so he stopped slicing his long shots. He played the new and better way for about a week, then changed back. "What happened to that grip I gave you?" I asked him on the practice tee one day. "That grip was fine, Sam," he replied, slicing another shot and then grinning at me like a monkey. "But I like my old grip better. This is *me!*"

Well, believe me, if your game is poor now, it isn't going to get much better unless you agree to make a few changes in it. Accept the fact that it's impossible to change anything without becoming a mite uncertain and nervous along the way. My friend decided he wanted no part of any suffering that he couldn't recognize, so he went back to playing with a God-awful grip—which was his right. But he also had to accept the penalty of a permanent slice.

Learning also has to come from the inside, or it won't stick, as exemplified by the time I took a woman of average strength and coordination, who'd never played golf before, and steered her around a golf course in under 100. I steered her through each and every setup and swing, and, of course, she shot the score with my feel and my knowledge, not her own. When she did go out on her own, she flopped. She had nothing inside to call on.

Something like that particular failure often seems to take place in players who are lured by all the new golfing "methods" that happen along. Actually, the fault lies not so much in the method as in the *attitude* of the golfer toward the method. You can't let a new golf method "happen" to you—in the manner you can lie back in the barber chair and let your hair get cut—because nothing lasting will come out of the learning experience. Your faults will grow back into your golf game just as surely as your hair grows back after a clipping.

So bear in mind, in reading this book, that building or rebuilding a golf swing takes a big commitment. You can't make some casual "wouldn't-it-be-nice" half-decision about where you'd like to go in the game and expect good results. Improvement takes time and patience and practice and desire, and none of it ever comes as easy as it looks. But that's how a sturdy, workable, lasting personal style in golf is achieved.

6

2: Why Technique Works Better Than Method

A free and simple approach to golf is more effective than a complicated method. For instance, when I swing at a golf ball right, my mind is blank and my body is loose as a goose.

That's not saying I haven't done a lot of thinking about my game, or worrying and wondering, like any other golfer who's human. I've put in my share of hours on the practice tee, and I've tossed and turned through enough dreams about shot-making technique to keep a team of high-priced psychiatrists busy for a year.

Nor am I saying my body doesn't jam up on me or get sluggish or cantankerous from time to time. I've made some high scores in my career, and lost touch with different parts of my game more often than I like to remember.

What I do mean is that, over the past nearly fifty years of playing top-flight competitive golf, it seems like my best results have always come when I'm hardly trying at all. At those times my mind and body go on automatic pilot, I swing with my smoothest rhythm and greatest vigor, and the birdie side of each hole opens up for me like I owned the course.

Now that's bad news to a certain kind of personality. There's a type of guy who'd rather hear that golf is hard work, period. He'd rather be told he needs a lot of muscle and a special method to get around in a fair score. Then he'll be able to go swing himself silly out on the golf course and feel like he's done a satisfying amount of hard labor.

Well, golf *is* hard work—but *not* on the golf course. It's hard work on the practice tee and on the practice putting green and in the practice bunker. The golf swing is a *learned* motion, an acquired habit. It's damn hard work thinking about what your swing really *feels* like, and where it could be improved, and what you have to do next to get yourself to play up to your potential. It's a form of self-knowledge, and that isn't easy to come by in any field. Like I said, the game is hard work—especially with the head.

As for "method," I'm afraid I've seen too many methods come and go in my half century in golf to really believe that the latest method on the market, whatever it may be, is going to solve anybody's golf problems for long. I'm not doubting the sincerity or professionalism of the proponents of these methods. As a matter of fact, I believe that even a poorly conceived method can indirectly help a certain type of golfer simply by getting him to think consciously about his game and about what it will take to improve it. On the other hand, I've seen too many fine players on tour lose their winning edge because of a sudden conversion to some method or other that, once mastered, supposedly guarantees never missing another fairway or green.

Here, maybe, is the nub. A cause-oriented method *explains* the golf swing, but doesn't make a good golf game happen. A sound, individualized, results-oriented *technique,* along with persistence and patience, does lead to a good game. And keeps the explanations down to a mouthful.

That said, let me try to keep *my* explanations short.

8

Let's go back now to what I said at the start of this chapter, which was that when I hit a golf ball right my mind is blank and my body is loose as a goose. What do I really mean by that?

MY MIND IS BLANK . . .

I don't go into a trance when I address the ball, but maybe I come close to that. I pull the plug out of the part of my brain where the conscious thinking is done, and all the words and thoughts and worries go down the drain. Nothing else exists. My mind is free of facts and fantasies about the past, present, and future, about my personal or business life, about my standing in the tournament at hand, and about the trees and traps along the hole I'm playing. If my mind isn't wrapped up in that moment—the way that mile-long thread of rubber is wrapped up inside the cover of the golf ball—then I'm going to make a mess of it.

When you stop to consider, it shouldn't be such a big deal to make your mind stand still for the few seconds it takes to get set and hit a golf shot. In a typical round, all that would be required would be five minutes or so of total concentration—certainly not enough to blow a mental fuse.

I think one reason many golfers have trouble achieving moments of total concentration is that they're too self-conscious; they can't seem to focus on something outside their personalities and identities, even for a few seconds at a time. They're like bad listeners. You often run into a fellow at a social gathering who can't hear a conversation without putting in his two cents' worth; he hasn't got the objectivity to stay quiet and maybe learn something. So a lot of good conversations never get finished. In the same way a lot of good golf swings never get made—because "garbage" butts in on the process.

"Garbage" is musing over the fifty-seven varieties of bad shots you might hit just now. It's also the word pros use for all kinds of extraneous thinking that goes on over the ball, such as how many points you lost on your favorite stock last week, or your opinion of your playing partner's orange slacks, or what you're planning to eat for supper later. You can live with a few ruined shots a round because of garbage. But if the condition gets to be chronic, you've got to do something about it—or give up the game. Because it isn't a game at that point, anyway—it's some kind of pointless exercise in self-abuse.

Another reason many golfers I've met can't achieve total concentration is because they're too brilliant for their own good. I know a fellow who's been taking expensive high-speed sequence photos of his swing for years, and using them to plot out how steep his swing plane is, how he should change his hand position at impact, and such. It's a form of self-knowledge, you might argue. Maybe so, and maybe it's useful knowledge to put to work on the practice tee. But whenever you bring this kind of mechanical information right up to the ball with you there's going to be trouble. After all these years my friend takes great photos—but he still can't swing the club worth a damn.

. . . AND MY BODY IS LOOSE AS A GOOSE

Tension is the product of technique or temperament, or both, and it just eats up the golf swing.

Without going into detail at this point, there is a big difference between my relatively free swing, which, "loose as a goose," minimizes tension, and the swings of some of my fellow tourists and numerous handicap golfers, where force, restriction, and inhibition seem to be at the core of the action.

With a forward press, a free arm swing, a fluid body turn, and good timing, the golf swing is a syrupy-smooth series of flowing actions. All the movements are, in fact, carefully controlled by a variety of factors built into the grip and stance and the hand-and-arm and body action. But within that framework the motion is free and flowing—smooth as pouring warm molasses.

There is a great gathering of force in the golf swing, to be sure, but it happens independently of any specific muscular movement you make. When I am trying for an extra-long drive, I actually feel I am taking the club back more *deliberately,* not with more strength. You hammer a tack home with a quick flick of the wrist. You drive a long spike by bringing that hammer up *deliberately*—gathering your power for a smooth, solid blow. The closest I come to feeling I am directly applying force in the golf swing is when I'm pouring it on with my right hand just before impact. But by this time my club head is on line and it is *flying*. The right hand, rather than foul anything up, is just going to slap more yardage into my shot.

The force-type swing tends to severely limit, or exaggerate, the participation of certain parts of the body. On tour, for example, certain players turn their shoulders fully but their hips hardly at all. What that does is coil a lot of leverage into the upper body muscles that can be delivered to the ball in the form of club head speed coming down. Fine. But the fact is that only the supple muscles of youth can repeatedly execute such a stressful action—and even then only after a lot of training. After thirty, that kind of backswing (in my kind both hips and shoulders turn in tandem) feels more like weight lifting than golf. And remember that anything based on tension, as this particular approach is, tends to dissolve in tension. When the chips are down, the force-type swing is not an easy swing to hold together, even for a youngster.

Another characteristic of the force-type swing on tour is excessive leg action. Certainly everybody's legs must *drive* their body weight into a full shot, and my legs are far from dormant in the golf swing. But in the free-type swing, the legs *pivot,* or *turn,* the body weight into the shot, an action that is more contained and easier to repeat year after year simply because it is less physically stressful. I'm in balance when I finish my swing, but relatively flatfooted. That shows I've contained my power.

I sometimes hear players of the force-swing school, on tour, talk about "working the club" up into such and such a position. Now that may be all right for a pro, who knows his swing as well as he knows the back of his hand, and so won't be susceptible to the negative import of such a phrase. But when the ordinary golfer starts thinking of his backswing as a species of manual labor—well, a whole lot of unnecessary huffing and puffing is going to appear in his game.

Incidentally, that "working the club" phrase points up the need for great care in selecting words and images to key your swing. I would never tell anyone to *work* the club up, for instance, because it creates an image of force. I'd tell them to *swing* the club up.

Of course, some of those fine young athletes out on the tour can do just about anything with their bodies and still make the golf swing work. But I, personally, believe that over the years the free-type swing has produced many more top players and consistent winners than the force-type swing. And I *know* that a freer swing would be better for the great majority of golfers who play, not for a living, but for pleasure.

The swing made freely is not only longer lasting than the force-type swing, since it involves less physical and mental wear and tear, but it is certainly one of the main reasons I'm still in the thick of things. It is also, swing for swing, a far more *enjoyable* experience when you're out on the golf course.

Controlled force in the swing of a touring pro can be effective within the limits I've mentioned. But in the swing of an ordinary player it is rarely productive. Hackers resort to force to minimize their errors, not to make the most of their strengths. A player may discover that squeezing the sawdust out of his club—exerting force through his grip—helps him keep his drives in the fairway. But generally he'll be paying a price for that accuracy, in the form of reduced wrist action, a sawed-off swing, and less yardage off the tee. Certainly he is not likely to be swinging in an arc that is as full and distance producing as it could be.

In various other ways—rigid legs, tight forearms, stiff backs, straining neck muscles—physical tension finds a place in the swings of players who have decided to force the golf ball into the air instead of letting it fly as the result of swinging freely. These golfers may have reduced, for the present, certain undesirable elements, like wildness. But they have also blocked their potential for future development. And they will probably not be able to contain that physical tension to one spot. Eventually it will creep into another part of the anatomy, cause yet another problem, and force the player to invent yet another improvised swing.

What about mental tension? We all know what it feels like to be tense or nervous, and we all *should* know how that can spoil performance. The person who is tense and self-conscious on the dance floor just plain can't dance. The rhythm and smoothness in the waltz, as in the golf swing, come from good timing. Unless you're nice and relaxed, good timing won't come, and you might as well sit out the dance—and the golf, too.

Mental tension destroys golfers for many reasons. If you don't have a technique you understand and a swing you can trust, you're bound to be nervous when you step up to the ball. If you're always thinking about results rather than performance, it's almost impossible not to feel tense, because your mind will dwell on the negative things like rough and hazards and out-of-bounds areas. If you're not sure what club to use in a certain situation, or have any other doubts, you will not be in a frame of mind to swing freely.

It's hard to separate mental tension from physical tension. One always leads to the other, with the result that your timing is thrown way off. And it's not something that you can get rid of all at once. It takes understanding to build confidence in your technique, and practice to build trust in your clubs. This game also takes an approach, on the course, that allows you to strip away every question mark about yourself and each shot as you come to it. All of that *frees* a man to do the best he can do.

Simplicity and freedom in the golf swing. That's what I mean when I say, "My mind is blank and my body is loose as a goose."

3: The Seven Traits You Want in Your Golf Swing

BEFORE we get into the mechanics of the game, I want to describe what I consider the outstanding qualities, or traits, in a good golfer.

These traits are rarely presented in a forthright manner in instruction books, simply because they are hard to pin down in words. Yet, understanding them—and getting them into your own game to the best of your ability—is crucial to making real progress in golf.

When, later on, we talk about the particular positions your hands and body should occupy at different points in the swing, or discuss any of the other myriad mechanical aspects of playing the game, bear in mind that, by trying always to acquire and hold these traits of good golf first, you will find it much easier to master the mechanical moves that come later.

There are seven traits in all: sensitivity, simplicity, harmony, smoothness, strength, directness, and style. They are the major factors for success in any swing, I think, and they are the marks of a real golfer.

14

SENSITIVITY: TUNE IN ON YOUR REAL SWING

Sensitivity means gauging what's really happening in your swing, and learning to tell the good, productive, dynamic feelings and effects from the bad ones. Awareness of your own physical strengths and weaknesses as they relate to swinging a golf club plays a big part in developing this kind of sensitivity.

This sensitivity may vary in people, but it is innate to the species, so most golfers have no excuse, except the excuse of laziness or indifference, for failing to tune in on their swings. When you do tune in, you start appreciating the *reality* of your game—the impact of a good shot on the forearm muscles, for instance, or the broken sound of a missed shot, or knowing if your hands are coming apart somewhere in the swing.

City people, as a rule, are stuck with a limited range of natural sounds and sights. Consequently, when they first get out into the country it takes time for their senses to tune in to the fact that there are a few million stars in the sky and a few hundred noises in the night air. A lot of golfers need to make a transition of a similar kind, to allow themselves to clearly perceive the working of their bodies during the swing.

SIMPLICITY: KEEP YOUR UNDERSTANDING ON A "NEED-TO-KNOW" BASIS

Simplicity is order and clarity in your thinking about golf. It's the opposite of the confusion I detect in so many club golfers. Once in a while I imagine stepping into the mind of a hacker trying to figure out the game without any help from a good teaching pro. I don't stay long, because it's like stumbling through the fun house at an amusement park —it's full of false paths and bumpy tracks and flashing signs and trick mirrors and muffled screams and all kinds of surprises popping out and attacking you.

The more the mind breaks down the swing intellectually, the more often your nerves break down trying to put it into action. So my own first principle has always been to make the game as simple as possible, both in understanding and in application. I limit myself to just a couple of keys, or conscious thoughts, at any one time in making the swing happen.

Now understand me clearly here. Simple doesn't mean stupid. I *do* have a very comprehensive and well-ordered mental picture of the golf swing, based on my own experience and on my observation of the five or six generations of golfers I've competed against. And I have a large body of knowledge about how the swing works physically—my "everyday information"—that I can draw upon when things go wrong. But the point is, *I never try to understand what I'm doing any more fully than I have to.* I never think about theory for the sake of thinking about it, only when I have to because something has gone wrong.

All my life I have tried to keep my swing as simple physically as my mental understanding of it. A good machine is one that's been designed to do all that it's supposed to do with no wasted power and no useless parts. The reason racers use a four-cylinder engine in cars in the Indianapolis 500 is because it is easier to fix and maintain than an eight-cylinder job. Same applies to the golf swing.

My swing doesn't have any little loops or lunges or flourishes—not because it's impossible to hit a good golf shot with such idiosyncrasies, but because they are not absolutely necessary. Learn to keep the moving parts down to the simplest possible minimum in the swing, and move those parts only where and when you have to, and you will develop an action that is economical, efficient, and easy to repeat.

HARMONY: UNITE "LEFT SIDE" AND "RIGHT SIDE"

Once you talk about the "parts" of a golf swing, you have to quickly mention the harmony of the parts or you're in trouble. As some golfer once said, the swing conceived in pieces is executed in pieces—and usually ends up in pieces.

Harmony is unity of action in the total golf swing. Harmony of mind and body. Harmony, within the mind, of conscious and unconscious. And, within the body, harmony of the opposite sides.

Many golfers think of their swings so completely in terms of left side vs. right side, left hand vs. right hand, and so on, that they're unable to achieve any kind of harmony at all. These actions eventually become a series of battles between various parts of their anatomy. Like Siamese twins trying to go in different directions, these golfers develop all kinds of painful stresses and strains in their bodies and their games.

There's no question but that, at different points in the swing, the left hand is more "active" or the right side is more "passive," and that every movement a golfer makes can be analyzed in those terms. Golf is such a highly specialized exercise, in fact, that I've found I can now reach up three inches higher on a wall with my left hand than with my right hand. Clearly my swing has required a lot more stretching by the left side of my body over the years than by the right side. Nonetheless, I have never thought of swinging with "a stretched left side," because I believe that would have deadened whatever is the equally important, though qualitatively different, simultaneous action of the right side. Instead, I've always thought of the left side and the right side participating fully in my swing, each in its own natural way.

Just by virtue of the grip and stance you assume to execute it, and

17

the equipment you use to do it with, the golf swing makes the opposite parts of the body behave automatically in different ways at different times—if you will allow them to, of course. A truly harmonious swing occurs when these opposites are resolved or balanced. For instance, the extension of my left side during a certain phase of the swing is balanced by a compression of my right side. But this is not something I need to analyze, or even think about. It's an *effect* of my swing pattern, not a *cause* of that pattern.

Ben Hogan used to practice the swing with his arms bound together by a belt around his forearms. He wasn't trying to stress the differing positions that the left arm and the right arm ideally occupy throughout the swing, but rather to encourage them to work in a balanced and thus a harmonious fashion.

I think of keeping my elbows together a lot, for the same reason. I also press my knees toward each other when I stand up to the ball, as though I'm slightly knock-kneed—again, in part, to help create a good working relationship between opposite sides.

If you think it will help you to understand, and when practicing emphasize, the different uses of the opposite sides of the body in the swing, go ahead. But remember that the full swing is made with the *whole* body. And its effectiveness depends in the final analysis on the harmony that can only come from a natural, balanced effort.

SMOOTHNESS: PUT THE WORDS TO MUSIC

Smoothness in the golf swing comes mainly from good timing or tempo, and I devote a chapter to that important subject later on. Basically, smoothness is the ability to perform all the varied actions of the swing in a sequence in which each one feeds and sustains all the others. You can learn by rote all the proper positions and individual movements theoretically necessary to strike a golf ball hard and true, but if you can't make them flow together your swing will be ineffective. A lot of golfers overreact to some of the standard teaching concepts in the game, which stress such things as the *straight* left arm, and the *straight* target line, and become so tensely perpendicular minded that their composure and fluid action is spoiled.

When you can perform the overall action with a sense and an appearance of rhythm, you usually have a payoff swing. It's all right to know the parts, but you've got to get them together, and in the right sequence. That's when you put the words to music.

STRENGTH: MUSCLES, WELL GOVERNED, PLAY A ROLE

You rarely hit a golf ball solidly when you're jumping at it—trying to let it all hang out. Club head speed isn't as great when you overexert, no matter how good bashing at the ball with all you've got may feel. I get my longest hits when I'm nice and relaxed and playing well within myself.

Having said that, I still want to stress that strength is a factor in golf. Swinging a golf club back and up, then down and through, is not like swatting flies. You're building and then applying leverage with that club, and it comes from muscle power.

I think too much emphasis has been placed on how easy and effortless the golf swing is supposed to be. I know the reason for this "go easy" emphasis is to get golfers to stop "killing the ball." But sometimes such advice gets a person so scrunched up and inhibited, or so dainty and ladylike, that he never makes a decent pass at the ball. Strength must be well governed and correctly applied in golf, through coordination and timing, but it should not be treated with disrespect or dragged from your game.

19

If you have a light grip on the club and a good, balanced stance, you'll come to no harm by hauling off on a shot, when extra distance is really necessary and prudent. Turning within your natural range of strength and suppleness will keep your muscles oiled and working well. Swinging so hard that you fall off balance or lose control of the club face is a problem. But holding back too much is also harmful.

It's my belief that strength is released through the nervous system acting on the muscles, rather than through the muscular system directly. I hit longer—outhit my normal distance with each club—when I'm in contention and the adrenaline is flowing, and that happens to all the pros. In fact, you can drop out of contention really fast when you're in this condition, if you don't club yourself extra carefully for each shot. Many a time on tour, players have found hazards or overhit greens just because they didn't figure in the added fifteen or twenty yards they're getting due to their charged-up state. Strength can hurt you when it takes you by surprise.

DIRECTNESS: PLAY WITHOUT PROCRASTINATING

The more direct, forthright, and orderly your approach to hitting a golf shot, the better your chances of success. I minimize the preliminaries to the swing just as I try to minimize the parts in the swing itself.

It's like trying to spell one of those long words out of the dictionary. Your first guess is usually your best, anyway. Once you stop to think it over, you're lost.

When you step up to the ball, you want to achieve three specific feelings: a sense of the target in relation to the ball, a sense of the ball in relation to your body, and a sense of the shot you intend to produce.

Therefore, you must develop a way to quickly and confidently "see" your target line. You must develop a pattern of stepping up to the ball that is functional and comfortable. And, finally, you must immerse yourself in the shot at hand, becoming conscious of the few—very few—specific bits of information you need to do the job, and oblivious to the many—very, *very* many—bits of information you don't need.

People without an organized or systematic approach to hitting a ball —and that covers most golfers, unfortunately—seem to fall into two camps. Some are impetuous, letting mood or emotion dictate how and what they do in preparation for each shot, and swinging as though the main idea is to get it over with as fast as possible. Others are more deliberate, but in a negative and inconsistent manner. They procrastinate, daydream, speculate, dawdle, fidget, worry, have second thoughts, and generally walk up to the ball as though it might explode. Actually, it usually fizzles.

In between is an approach that organizes the player's resources in the measure required to do the job. A systematic approach to shot making allows you to seize the moment of the swing with an intense gathering of all your faculties.

STYLE: FIND THE SWING THAT FEELS "YOU"

A golf swing is like a fingerprint, identifying its owner and also telling a bit about what that person is like. In all the years I've played and taught, I don't think I've ever seen two swings exactly alike.

Physical and temperamental factors create some of the differences. A short, fat fellow, for instance, naturally swings on a flatter plane and with a shorter arc than a lanky golfer. An excitable kind of guy naturally swings faster than a placid individual. A golfer with very strong hands or powerful legs will automatically put his natural advantage to work in the swing in various ways. An aggressive person will tend to hit with his hands, whereas a more timid fellow will depend on his body turn to generate power.

Other differences in style come from the random nature of the learning process. Chance and odd elements in each player's background sometimes stamp a golf game with a very noticeable strength or weakness. For instance, Jimmy Demaret's great short game came from hours of fooling around with touch shots as a kid in the caddie yard.

A good player goes with the type of swing that will work for him most consistently, no matter what it looks like or how hard it may be to execute. Thus there is no end of peculiarities on tour. Lee Trevino looks like he's aiming 45 degrees left of target when he stands up to the ball. Watch his swing and not where the shot goes and you'd guess he couldn't break 90! Jack Nicklaus and Gay Brewer play with a flying right elbow on their backswings. Miller Barber does a loop-the-loop in his swing that makes you dizzy.

A good player will also violate any golfing maxim, no matter how old and respected it might be, if it doesn't prove itself in performance. For Gary Player, for example, the maxim "Keep your left arm straight but not stiff" just never held water. Player's left arm always had a pronounced "give" at the elbow at the top. Of course at the bottom his left arm is firm as a steel girder.

The list of eccentricities in style, or departures from norm, is practically endless among good players, and it suggests that individual style in golf is not only inevitable but desirable. Learning to play golf well becomes largely a search for your own personal style.

"Okay, Sam," you might say. "How relevant is your style to mine?" Well, let's be honest about that. No swing can be Xeroxed—no swing can be transferred from one person to another without some modification. That's why there's so much variety around, as I mentioned.

My own swing has been used a lot as a model mainly because it is simple and smooth and relatively free of idiosyncrasy. It originates out of an orthodox grip and stance—a better word than orthodox might be "neutral"—neither of which I have had to tamper with in any significant way since I first put my game together.

My swing plane—the line on which I draw the club up and then down—is about as simple as you can make it. One of my main swing thoughts has always been to swing the club back down to the ball on the same line that I carry it back and up from the ball, and through years of practice I've come pretty close to that goal. The similarity between my backswing and downswing planes is actually what gives observers the impression of "smoothness" in my action.

The position of my hands at the top of my swing—that crucial position from which the hitting phase of the swing is launched—is what I would call "neutral." That is, my hands are positioned about midway between my head and my right shoulder before I begin the downswing. Golfers whose builds dictate swinging in a more upright plane—a plane closer to vertical than horizontal—would normally reach the top with the hands closer to the head. Golfers with flatter or more horizontal swings would swing their hands up nearer to the shoulder. The position of my hands is in between those two extremes.

Such features have made my golf swing "transferrable," though not in a way that would restrict an individual from developing according to his or her particular build and personality.

If a person wants to build a house economically, he usually looks for a building site that needs a minimum of clearing or other costly modifications. In that sense, my swing might be analogous to an acre of desirable real estate. You can copy it more easily than many other swings —you can set your house on it cheaply. And at the same time you can develop those mannerisms that come out of your own uniqueness—you can make a house a home.

This swing of mine came to have an easy-to-copy quality, I think, because when I set out to build a golf game—untutored, as I mentioned earlier—I worked from results backwards. I had no preconceived notions of form when I began. My only desire was to hit the ball hard and long, and reasonably straight. If it had been necessary for me to swing with one foot in the air, or with both eyes closed, I probably would have done that. I let *results* impose form on my swing, rather than theory or style or any other factor.

And that's how it became, in time, closer to an "ideal" than most.

Part II
FOUNDATIONS

4: How to Groove a Swing That's Right for You

THE main purpose of this book is to help you find the stroke within yourself—the way of swinging a golf club that's suited to your particular build, strengths, and temperament—the stroke that will allow you to compete effectively on the golf course.

In order to be effective, no matter what you're like physically, this stroke must deliver your club approximately square to your ball and target, and at a good rate of speed—and it must do so time after time. In other words, what we're after is a repeating swing that produces maximum distance with maximum accuracy. When you come right down to it, having grooved their swings—having achieved "repeatability"—is what separates good golfers from the pack.

My suggested approach to grooving a swing, in capsule form, is as follows:

1. Acquire the foundations of holding the club and standing to ball and target correctly.

2. Use hand action "keys" to develop a full swing arc and the proper

"NEUTRALITY" OF GRIP

Most good golf grips fall somewhere between the "strong" grip of Billy Casper and the "weak" grip of Johnny Miller. My own grip is between those two extremes, a shade on the strong side. The majority of golfers are better off with the more in-between or neutral grip, in my opinion, because it reduces the tendency of the hands to over-manipulate the club during the swing. Some of the pros can handle extremes in their grips and swing effectively. But the average golfer with a very strong or weak grip will tend to turn and twist the club excessively during the swing, and thus greatly reduce his chances for consistency.

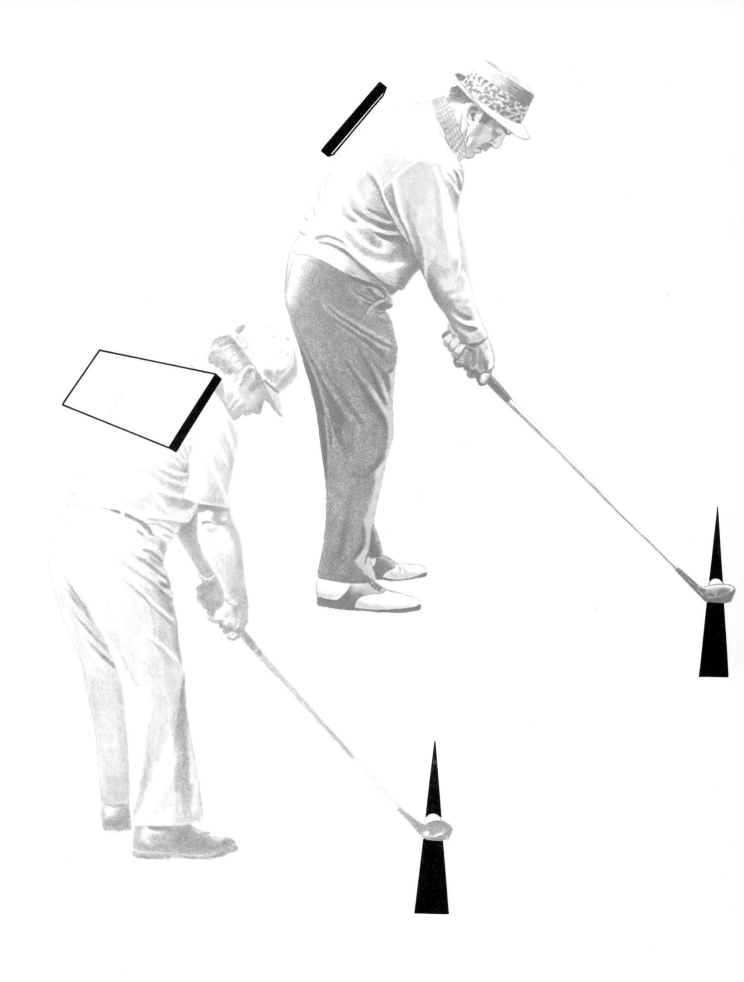

"NEUTRALITY" OF STANCE

The best golfing stance to start with is a "comfortably square" stance such as mine, with shoulders and feet set on a line that is close to parallel to the target line. Winning swings can be developed with an extremely open stance, such as the slightly exaggerated one Lee Trevino is shown in, or with a closed stance such as the one Frank Beard here occupies. But many golfers don't have the inborn skills or the available practice time to mold a consistent swing on an unusual stance. The more orthodox stance helps the average golfer to draw the club head back along the target line, and to swing it through the ball along the target line. That spells squarer hits more of the time.

wrist action needed to generate club-head speed.

3. Use posture and body-movement "keys" to build a balanced turn to support the arc of the swing through the action of the hands.

4. Build your timing to get the hands, body, and club head working together.

5. Practice the swing until it becomes a habit of mind and muscle.

This approach in all its stages will be detailed in later chapters. After that, I will present some specific ideas on cutting strokes from your score during actual play, in chapters on tactics, the short game, and the mental and emotional traits you need to win at golf.

At this point I would like to suggest how my approach might best fit into your present golfing experience and development.

Whether you're a beginner or an experienced player trying to overcome bad habits, the job of grooving a swing has to be done patiently, and in stages. Let me explain generally what I see as a good, methodical way of grooving a swing, and point out the main things you should strive for at each stage.

During the first stage, you should practice with short clubs—nothing longer than the seven iron—(1) to develop and get used to a correct grip, and (2) to develop a feeling for the action positions of the hands in the swing. Chipping short shots toward a target in your back yard or garage, or hitting longer chips and pitches at a practice area, are two good starting points.

During the second stage, you should gradually extend your swing by using longer clubs—up to the 4 iron, say—and by concentrating on producing a consistent *arc* in the trajectory of the shots you hit. By arc, I mean the height at which your ball travels, which is the product of the angle of the loft of the club at the moment the club meets the ball. If you can achieve the same arc, or height, on a series of shots hit with the same club, even though distance and direction in these shots may greatly vary, it means that your swing motion is becoming grooved.

During the third stage, you should continue to use primarily the medium irons to work at achieving better directional—side-to-side—control over your shots by making use of selected body keys and by building your timing. This is probably the most frustrating stage in a golfer's development because some of the keys just won't work for him —or will open the wrong doors and present him with previously unknown faults. That's why, during this stage, it's important to go back to Stage One, from time to time, to *resimplify* your swing.

During the final stage, you should extend your swing to its fullest by moving on to your driver and the other wood clubs, and by concentrating on producing a consistent *curve* in the trajectory of the shots you hit. By curve, I mean the direction in which the ball turns—to the left or to the right—in flight, which is the product of the interrelationship between the path of the club head and the direction in which the club face is looking at the moment of impact. Shots with the longest clubs curve most, because the comparatively steep faces of these clubs puts relatively little backspin on the ball, so that any sidespin produced by the club face looking to left or right during impact has a relatively large influence on the flight of the ball.

When you can achieve pretty much the same curve on a series of shots hit with the driver, it means your swing is almost fully grooved. More practice, and perhaps a slight modification in grip or stance, is, then, all that is needed to finally groove a swing and a shot pattern that will make you highly effective on the golf course.

Of course, none of the above is as easy as I have made it sound. In fact, the majority of average players never get to the fourth and final stage of achieving a constant shot pattern—of hitting drives that consistently curve in flight either to the right or to the left—simply because they are not prepared to commit the time, sweat, and careful self-observation to the job of becoming a real golfer.

That's why I'd like to emphasize, at this point, the value of having specific, clear goals along the road to achieving the ultimate goal of the game, which is a repeatable shot pattern. That way, there is a better

'NEUTRALITY' OF SWING PLANE

The golfer's position at the top—the all-important power slot in golf—is the tip-off on the type of swing plane he has. In his later years, Ben Hogan was famous for bringing the club up in a very flat plane. Jack Nicklaus, by contrast, swings the club back on a much more upright plane. My own position at the top is about midway between these two extremes. I figure my left arm swings back into the space between my head and shoulder at an angle of about 45°. Physique plays a role here. It's natural for the short and/or heavy-set person to stand a bit farther from the ball, and so to swing the club around his body in a flatter plane; and for the lanky type to stand closer to the ball and so to swing the club on a more upright angle. Speaking generally, more golfers will develop the swing plane that is most natural for them—and therefore most effective for their golf games—by swinging back to a comfortable intermediate position at the top, rather than copying some extreme position that has worked for another player.

chance that you will be encouraged to persist in your efforts to arrive at Stage Four.

First of all, there is an important *strategic* reason for building yourself a predominant shot pattern, that is, a swing that consistently produces a ball that curves either slightly from *right to left* in flight, known as a "draw," or a ball that curves slightly from *left to right*, known as a "fade."

The reason is: *It cuts your margin for error in half.*

Let me explain. When you are confident in the type of curve you are going to produce, you can set up to the ball and aim your shots in a manner that virtually eliminates the potential trouble on one side of the golf course. For example, if there is a pond or stream on the right side of the fairway, aiming your draw to start out along that side will bring the ball into the fairway well left of the trouble. Or, suppose you

are a fader faced with a long approach shot to a green where the pin is guarded on the right front side by bunkers. You can then aim to fly the ball into the green on the left side, thus avoiding going over the trap, and let the fade spin on the ball move it into the area where the flagstick sits.

In other words, by having a definite curve pattern in your swing, you can always hit the ball so that it will "bend" *away from*, rather than *toward,* severe trouble areas. And in many cases you will be able to minimize the risk of intervening hazards in trying to place the ball close to well-guarded pin positions.

If you have an *indefinite* curve pattern in your swing, however, your chances of placing the ball effectively will be pretty slim in situations where accuracy is a must. Not knowing whether you're going to draw or fade the ball, you are almost always certain to try to steer the shot.

STEPS TO GROOVING A SWING

Grooving the Hand Action (7-iron)
The starting point for grooving (or re-grooving) a swing should be concentrated practice of little shots with a short iron. Set up a 10- or 15-yard range in your backyard with an old piece of carpet for your turf and a pail or basket for your target. Work on the short chip shots to build up your knowledge of what the hands actually do during the swing.

Applying the Body Keys (5-iron)
The 5-iron is my favorite practice club because it is long enough to build my pivot and short enough to be manageable even on a bad day. It's the club to use in developing and grooving the key body actions.

Blending Hand Action and
Body Keys through Timing (driver)
The ultimate test of a golf swing is how it performs with the No. 1 wood. If your timing is right, your hand action and body movements will work together to make that big club head fly into the ball at the bottom of your arc with power to spare.

Do that and all rhythm and coordination, not to mention distance, disappear.

That brings me to the big *physical* reason for building a predominant shot pattern, which is that it is much too hard to hit a golf ball perfectly straight, anyway. Why? Well, let's look at it in terms of the geometrical factors involved. To hit the ball straight—absolutely dead straight, I mean—the club head must be traveling *exactly* along that target line during the millisecond of impact, and its face must be looking *exactly* at the target. Only then is the ball given the spin that is necessary for it to fly dead straight.

To do that repeatedly, at the 100-mph-plus speeds necessary to hit the ball far, is beyond any mortal's capacity. Thus, even the greatest golfers accept the fact that they are bound to hit "across" the ball *very slightly* from one side of the target line or the other, which means that they will always tend to impart some small degree of sidespin to the ball.

If they hit across the ball very slightly from beyond (outside) the target line, with the club face pointing at the target (making it in actual fact "open"—facing to the right of—their swing path), then they will impart the slight left-to-right sidespin to the ball that produces the fade. If they hit very slightly across the ball from the near side (the "inside") of the target line, with the club face pointing at the target (making it in fact slightly "closed"—facing to the left of—their swing path), then they will impart the slight right-to-left sidespin that produces the draw. (Let me just interject here that the only difference "geometrically" between the good golfer's fade or draw and the hacker's big slice or hook is the hacker's bigger angle at impact between club head path and club face alignment. In other words, the slicer is coming from way "outside," with the club face looking way right of target, and the hooker is coming from way "inside," with the club face looking way left of target.)

Why not develop both the draw and the fade?

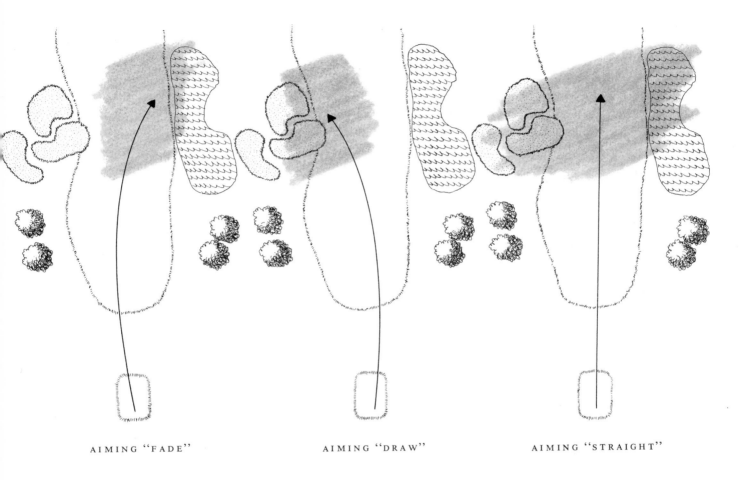

AIMING "FADE"   AIMING "DRAW"   AIMING "STRAIGHT"

WHY A RELIABLE SHOT PATTERN PAYS OFF

It doesn't make sense to try to hit perfectly straight shots in golf for the mechanical reason that it is physically impossible to deliver the club head to the ball dead center all the time, and for the strategic reason that you invite double the trouble when you do aim "straight." Note in our hole diagrams how the would-be straight-shooter risks catching the water on his right or the bunkers on his left, since, with no controlled shot pattern, his drives are likely to veer to either side of the fairway. But the player with a grooved left-to-right fade pattern, or right-to-left draw pattern, actually eliminates one side of the fairway from his possible landing area and thus cuts in half his chances of hitting into trouble.

Idealistically, one might argue that both types of curve should be within the capability of every golfer, because just about every golf course demands both types of curves, for driving the ball to the best fairway positions and for getting it close to elusive pin placements on the greens.

Realistically, however, trying to curve balls at will in either direction is a massive obstacle to developing a grooved swing. In the early stages, a golfer's main concern must be to develop a swing pattern that feels natural to him within the limits of the hand actions and body movements that are the key to all good swings, and which I prescribe in detail later on. Trying to control, precisely, the pattern of flight of shots *before* the hand actions and body movements have begun to harmonize results in a swing that is overmechanical in that it is overcontrolled—usually by artificial manipulation of the hands or overdeliberate "positioning" of the bodily components.

Keep clearly in your mind that, in a good draw or fade swing, the angle at which the club head approaches the ball, whether from inside or outside the line, is never severe. In fact, for the practical purposes of all but the most advanced golfers, the club head should be thought of as traveling exactly along the line to the target the instant before, of, and after impact. Trying to overprecisely "angle" the club head into the ball in your developmental stage is like trying to park a Mack truck in your first driving lesson. At best it will yield the extreme versions of each type of curve—a duck hook instead of a draw, and a banana-ball slice instead of a fade—while preventing you from developing a smoothly natural set of hand and body swinging actions.

Another reason I object to trying to develop a certain shot pattern prematurely is that it takes the golfer's mind off the swing and puts it on the shot. Beginners who concentrate on *where* they're hitting, instead of *what* they're hitting, are usually the ones who develop the kinks and loops and inhibitions that spoil so many swings and limit so much golfing potential.

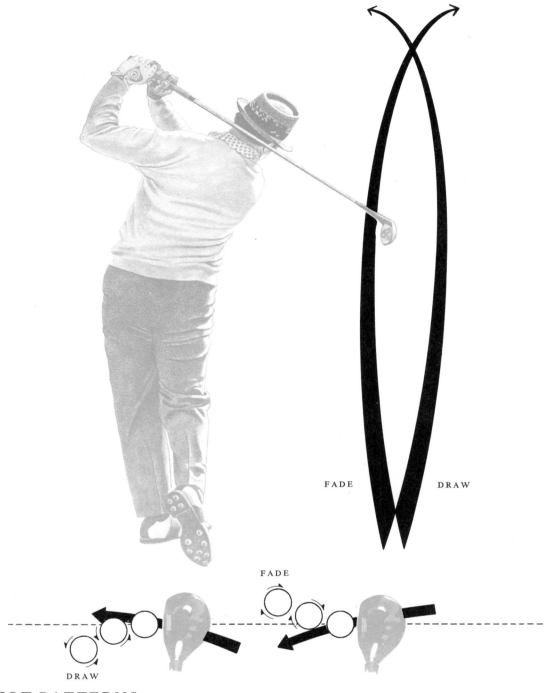

FADE

DRAW

FADE

DRAW

SHOT PATTERNS

The stock-in-trade of all good golfers is a reliable shot pattern, either a fade that flies left to right (a manageable version of the hated slice) or a draw that flies right to left (a modified hook). Top golfers can produce either type of shot at will but generally find one or the other more reliable or personally easier to play as a bread-and-butter shot. The shots curve in their particular flight pattern because of the type of spin imparted when the club head brushes against the ball during impact.

Once you have built a consistent swinging motion, and are producing shots with consistent arcs, you can pick the predominant shot pattern for your game. But, by that time, if you have grooved your swing properly, your shot pattern will actually have picked you, largely on the basis of your individual build and strengths. The stronger and more competitive player will usually tend to develop a draw-producing swing, while the physically weaker or "play-for-fun" golfer will usually settle for a fade. In both cases, of course, what we're aiming for is a *slight* curve to the shot—not the violent banana balls that characterize the games of most weekend golfers.

Each type of shot pattern has advantages. The draw produces more distance because the club head hits the ball more solidly in back in moving lower to the ground as it travels from the inside, and the ball also backspins less with draw spin applied and so jumps forward more from the bounce. The fade makes up in control for the ten to fifteen yards that it loses in distance (comparing the typical drives of a good fade player and a good draw player). It is especially valued for its quick "stopability" (due to greater height and backspin) on narrow fairways and hard or fast greens.

My main point is that your natural shot pattern is the one you should permit to develop, because, whether it be fade or draw, it is the shape that will lead to a repetitive and longer-lasting swing for you person-ally.

In time, once you have a solid swing that consistently slightly fades or draws your shots, you may choose to introduce minor variations in stance to produce the opposite curve, or to accentuate your usual curve. A more closed alignment of feet and shoulders at address will encourage an inside-out, or draw, swing; a more open-address setup, an outside-in, or fade, swing. Eventually, you may even learn to vary the shape of your shots without making any alterations in setup—as I do —but simply by making up your mind to produce one curve or the other, and letting your well-trained golfing reflexes subtly alter your hand and body action during the impact zone to produce the desired "shape."

But, for most golfers, such finesse should be a distant goal at best. Grooving the swing comes first. And that means, to start with, building the foundations of your grip and setup . . .

5: How to Build Your Grip

GRIPPING a golf club is a highly specialized action, like nothing else you do. The hands must be set around the club handle, and in relation to each other, in a way that is not quite so easy and natural as some people might think. In fact, most weekend golfers—I venture to say as many as nine out of ten—have terrible grips. Their fingers resemble bananas on a vine, or snakes in a pit, more than human hands arranged to perform a delicate feat of speed and precision.

A good grip helps shape a swing correctly, and it influences the overall *tone* of the swing—its rhythm and smoothness. A bad grip contains the seeds for all kinds of fearsome swing problems. No other sound action position of the hands—and sometimes not even of the body—can be properly and easily achieved when you start out with a bad grip. What results instead is a variety of short-term cures and compensations that cut your golfing potential practically in half.

Building a good grip takes a fair amount of conscious fidgeting and patient practice, until it begins to feel halfway comfortable. But, once it is achieved, the payoff is handsome and long lasting.

When assumed correctly, the grip creates a kind of balance of power

44

between your left hand and your right hand, so that the two hold and move the club in a coordinated, unified action. The pain and strife of a long marriage, or a tricky business merger, might thus be said to be analogous to the trouble of developing a good grip. But so are the pleasures and the profits.

Taking the little finger of the right hand off the club entirely is one way that power is balanced in the grip; with one less finger in the action, the right hand automatically becomes less involved and influential. The great British champion Harry Vardon popularized this device by laying the little finger of his right hand on top of the forefinger of his left hand, as a result of which the grip came to be known as the "Vardon overlap." To this day it is the most widely used grip among good players, and the one most commonly taught on the nation's lesson tees.

A later variation of the overlap involved the entwining or interlocking of the same two fingers—the little finger of the right hand with the forefinger of the left hand—and produced the same power-balancing, hands-unifying result. A few golfers with small hands—notably Gene Sarazen and Jack Nicklaus among pros—have found this form of marrying the hands most comfortable for them and just as effective as the overlap, and you've nothing to lose by giving it a try, especially if you have small or weak hands.

Whether achieved by overlapping or interlocking, the correct grip limits the stronger, dominant hand just enough to bring the two hands into balance. And, just as important, this meshing of the hands brings them snugly together on the club handle, thus encouraging a more uniform, blended action throughout the swing.

Now let me explain, precisely, how to assume the correct grip, and describe the feeling you should seek in this first action position of the hands. (If you're a lefty, reverse all instructions.)

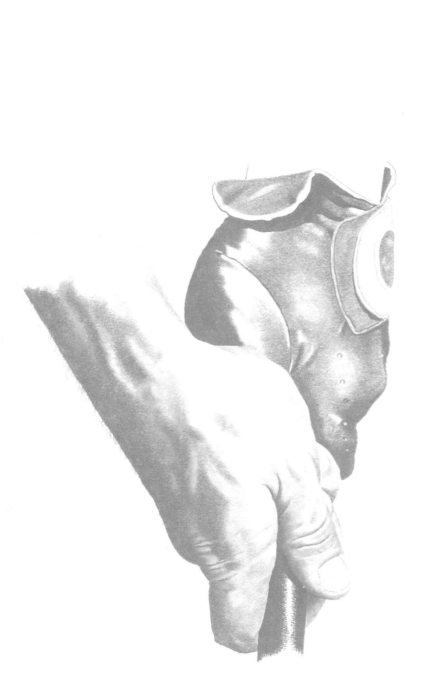

GRIP—FIRM BUT FLEXIBLE

A snug grip that gives you control over the golf club without inhibiting fluid hand and wrist action at any point in the swing is the basic of all the basics in golf. A good way to ensure control plus flexibility is to make sure that you maintain three pressure points in your hands 1) at the top of the grip, by squeezing with the last two fingers of your upper hand 2) in the middle, by interlocking or overlapping the little finger of your lower hand and 3) at the bottom of your grip by firmly "pinching" the club handle with the thumb and forefinger.

THE LEFT-HAND GRIP

The left-hand grip is a butt-and-finger grip. Sole the club level on the ground and let its handle rest diagonally across the fingers and palm of your left hand. Next, wrap your fingers around the club so that the thumb rides comfortably just off the top of the shaft, and the V-shaped crease formed by the thumb and forefinger points toward your right shoulder. Now, to create the proper control over the club, get a solid purchase on the target side of the handle with some of that fatty tissue in the heel or butt of your hand, and apply a bit of squeeze with the last two fingers on the other side of the shaft. Those two small actions box in the club handle snugly, so that it won't come loose at any point in the heat of the swing. But check to see that the shaft is really firmly boxed in by extending the club in the air before you and holding on without using your thumb. That's the kind of security and control you must have in the left-hand grip.

THE RIGHT-HAND GRIP

The right-hand grip is almost entirely a finger grip. Encircle the club shaft with your right hand and slide it snugly up next to your left hand, letting your thumb ride comfortably across the top of the handle, and making sure the V-shaped crease formed by the thumb and forefinger of this hand also points toward your right shoulder. Your right little finger overlaps (or interlocks with) the forefinger of the left hand on the underside of the club handle. Your right forefinger and thumb should press upon the club handle in a kind of "pinch," and as a result there will be a slight gap or separation between the forefinger and the other fingers. The security and control in the right-hand grip comes from this "pinch," and from the firm marriage of the right little finger to the left forefinger through the overlap or interlock.

Looking down at your hands set together on the club handle at this point, double-check the V-shaped creases formed by the thumbs and forefingers. The creases should be parallel, and should point directly over your right shoulder. You should also feel, again, the "boxing in" action of the left hand at the top of the shaft, the overlapping or inter-locking of both hands at the middle, and the "pinching in" action of the right hand at the bottom.

Control of the club handle is thus established without undue appli-cation of pressure through the hands, ensuring that the wrists will hinge freely at all times. Too much overall pressure would tend to lock your wrists and greatly inhibit your swing.

ALIGNMENT OF THE HANDS

When the V-shaped creases are pointing to your right shoulder, and the three key pressure points in your grip are operative, your grip will be in a plane that is what I would call "comfortably square" to your target. That means that the back of your left hand and the palm of your right hand will be facing pretty much toward the target—or, at worst, a little to the right of target.

It's important to be aware of this grip plane, simply because it can shift or tilt subtly without your noticing. When that happens, the hands will involuntarily want to manipulate the club at some point in the swing, in attempted compensation for their incorrect alignment at the outset.

The grip plane can become distorted by a change in position of either hand or both hands. A common error is for one or both hands to tilt back, away from the target—the right hand slipping partly under the club handle and the left hand tending to ride atop the shaft. This is called a "strong" grip, because the hands are more behind the ball and convey a greater sense of strength and power to the unsophisticated player.

Many youngsters and women naturally assume such a grip, their lack of hand and arm strength encouraging them to position their hands more behind the club, in an effort both to control the club and to get the sensation that they can hit powerfully with it.

Many golfers who do possess the necessary hand and arm strength assume too-strong grips if and when they discover that this style of grip can help them to cut down on their slicing. That happens because the right hand, in trying, involuntarily, to get back to "square," turns over the left hand during the downswing and closes the club face, which either pulls or hooks the ball to the left. Of course, you should never

"IMPOSSIBLE" POSSIBLE PREFERRED

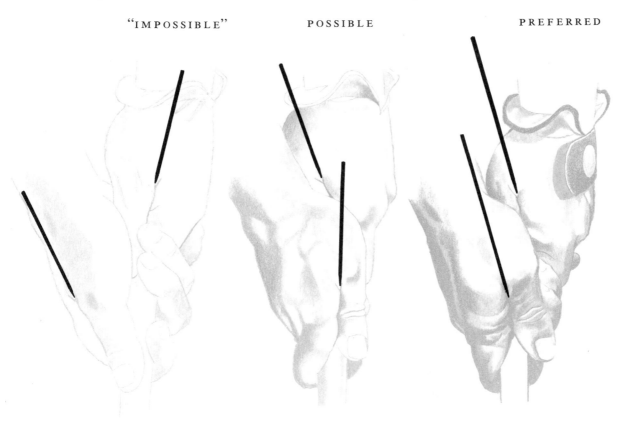

Both hands must work together as a unit in golf, or the swing suffers. Setting the hands in opposition to each other, with the upper hand weak and the lower hand strong, creates a gap between the hands and virtually guarantees a chaotic swing. Setting the upper hand comparatively strong and the lower hand weak is workable, because the hands are brought very snugly together in the grip. But a more natural grip for most golfers is the slightly strong grip in which the Vs of both hands point to the right shoulder.

correct what is basically a swing problem with a change in grip—or, for that matter, what is a grip problem with a change in swing—but the average player makes many such compensations without really being aware that he is making them. That's the main reason he's so inconsistent.

In what is known as a "weak" grip, the left hand sits partly under the club handle and the right hand tends to ride atop the club. The inclination of a player with a weak grip is to bring his club into the ball with the face open, which happens because, during the stress of swing motion, his hands tend to revert instinctively to normal (square) by impact. The result is a push or slice.

A few top golfers have successfully balanced out the tendency of the right hand to overpower the left by setting the left hand in a normal position and the right hand in a comparatively weak position—in fact, Walter Hagen and Bobby Jones both played this way with great success, as does Johnny Miller today. But the reverse never works. Setting the left hand in a weak position and the right in a strong position sets the hands totally in opposition to each other, usually creates a gap between them, and, all in all, tends to encourage the gorilla species of golf swing.

6: How to Set Up and Aim Correctly

A good golf stance sets your body, club, and ball in a relationship to one another that makes it possible for you to hit the ball:

1. In balance (that is, when you are fully in control of your physical movements)—for *consistency*.

2. At or fractionally before the lowest point of your swing arc, when the club head is traveling directly *forward* (that is, not sharply down or up)—for *power*.

3. In the direction of your target (that is, when your swing arc momentarily coincides with your target line)—for *accuracy*.

Let's now look at this correlation in more detail. I think doing so will help you to see the truth of the old saw that good golf starts at ground level, and also make it easier for you to understand the real reasons why your stance must vary according to the type of shot you are seeking to play.

CONSISTENCY THROUGH BALANCE

The need to achieve consistency through balance is built into the stance by a relaxed and fairly upright posture, which is the only posture that will hold up under the pressure of action. For instance, if you crouch too much at address, you'll tend to straighten up during the swing and alter the line along which the club head is moving. If you stand too straight, you'll tend either to crouch or to fall back as the action develops.

You should also stand as *close* to the ball as you can without interfering with a free and comfortable swing action.

Most golfers tend to stand too far from the ball, because doing so gives them a sense of having "more room to operate." Actually, what reaching does is limit your ability to fully use your legs and body in the swing. Most golfers who reach for the ball at address tend to throw the club from the top with their hands and arms during the downswing. The body is positioned too far away to coil properly in the backswing and to shift effectively in the downswing, and as a result the shot is weakly executed with hands and arms only.

Another aid to balance is to stand up to the ball with your feet turned outward in a natural manner—the way they would be if you were just standing in an ordinary relaxed position. Don't try to put either foot perpendicular to the target line—the imaginary straight line running from ball to target. Remember, you're not a diagram. If your feet aren't comfortable, tension will build up in them and in your calf muscles and might even spread into your knees.

Finally, the feet should be relatively close together—closer than most golfers tend to place them in the stance—to provide the foundation for a nice, balanced pivot. For the driver swing, the feet should be no farther apart than the width of your shoulders, and for the short irons half that distance. A lot of golfers assume too wide a stance because it gives them a feeling of great power and stability. Actually, a too-wide stance tends to shorten the backswing and reduces power instead of increasing it. A wide stance also encourages swaying and moving off the ball. A narrower stance centers your body weight better at the start and tends to keep it centered throughout the swing. It also encourages you to turn more fully and with less effort, both going back from and coming through the ball, which is imperative to both power and accuracy.

Those are my main thoughts on a balanced golfing posture. I'll have more to say about the mechanics of posture in the chapter on body keys.

POWER AND STANCE

The need to generate power affects the stance in two important ways.

First, the bigger the shot, the broader the *base* you need (within the limits set by your need for balance), because the relatively large and complex body action inherent in a full swing effort demands a more solid platform than is needed for a little shot, which is played more with the hands and arms and less with the body. It follows, then, that for the driver (which normally has a shaft length of forty-three inches) your feet are farther from each other, and from the ball itself, than with any other club. Your feet are closest to each other, and to the ball, on shots made with the pitching wedge (which usually measures around thirty-one inches).

Second, the bigger the shot the more weight you need *behind* the ball as it is struck. It follows, then, that for the drive the ball should be positioned fairly well forward in the stance—about opposite your left heel—so you are looking at the back of the ball out of your left eye. For the little pitch or chip, where control is more important than power, the ball is positioned in the middle of the narrower stance, and your head (and thus your eyes) is more directly over rather than behind, the ball.

53

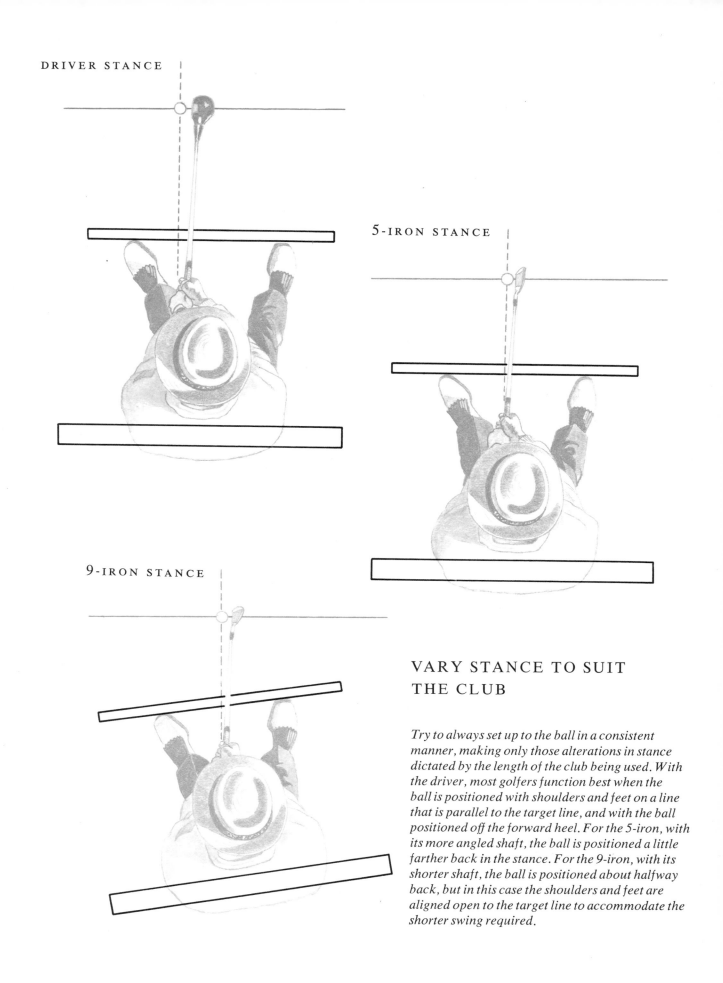

DRIVER STANCE

5-IRON STANCE

9-IRON STANCE

VARY STANCE TO SUIT THE CLUB

Try to always set up to the ball in a consistent manner, making only those alterations in stance dictated by the length of the club being used. With the driver, most golfers function best when the ball is positioned with shoulders and feet on a line that is parallel to the target line, and with the ball positioned off the forward heel. For the 5-iron, with its more angled shaft, the ball is positioned a little farther back in the stance. For the 9-iron, with its shorter shaft, the ball is positioned about halfway back, but in this case the shoulders and feet are aligned open to the target line to accommodate the shorter swing required.

I never position the ball back of center in my stance except for unusual shots, such as when I'm playing from a severe downhill or sidehill lie. So, in fact, the range in ball position in my stance is only a matter of a few inches up and down the target line—from a point opposite my left heel back to a point opposite the center of my stance. For drives and fairway woods, I play the ball from the forward position, off the left heel. For irons one through four, I play the ball between the heel and the center, or midpoint, of my stance. And for all other clubs, from the five iron through the wedges, I play the ball in the center of my stance.

Don't stray dramatically from these ball-position guidelines in grooving your swing, and take care, especially, not to play shots too far *forward* of the positions I've suggested for the various clubs. Largely because almost all golfers slice, they involuntarily tend, in their attempts to stop the ball going to the right, to move the ball farther forward in relation to their feet as they aim their feet and shoulders more and more to the left. This is actually the *exact reverse* of what they should do to stop slicing, as we shall see shortly.

ACCURACY THROUGH BODY ALIGNMENT

Accuracy is built into the stance by lining up your feet and your shoulders in a specific relationship to the target line—that imaginary straight line running through the ball to your target.

Now, body alignment is something that, after fifty years in the game, I personally do not have to think about consciously when I address a shot. In my case, my upper-body alignment automatically matches the alignment of my feet as I set up to each shot. Thus, if I stand square in my feet, my shoulders will also be square; if I stand open in my feet, my shoulders will also be open; and if I stand closed in my feet, my shoulders will be equally closed. But I want to emphasize here the strong influence of upper-body alignment as well as feet alignment on shot pattern, because for many handicap golfers it is the root of a lot of the stubborn slices and hooks one sees on every golf course.

The best policy in developing a solid, full, swing pattern is to stand *square* to your target line in both your feet and your shoulders. Theoretically, at least, this gives you the best chance of instinctively delivering the club head to the ball at impact, while it is momentarily traveling along the target line.

Once you have grooved your swing, your square alignment need never change—unless you wish to alter your basic shot pattern to meet the needs of on-course strategy. In such cases, all that is necessary to produce the two basic flight patterns of fade and draw is to aim your grooved swing according to how you want the ball to fly.

Thus, if you want the ball to *fade,* all you need do is simply aim both your feet and shoulders a little to the *left* of target. Then, however, *you must make certain to swing along the line of your body alignment,* and *not* along your direct ball-to-target line. This will have the effect of delivering the club head to the ball traveling slightly across the target line from the outside. The ball will then start to the left, in the direction the club head is traveling. However, because of the brushing action of the square-to-target club face across the ball from right to left, sidespin will be imparted that curves the ball back to target. There, as simply as possible, is your fade.

If you want the ball to *draw,* simply aim your feet and shoulders a little to the *right* of target. Again, *you must make absolutely certain that you then swing along the line established by your feet and shoulders,* and *not* along the direct ball-to-target line—in other words, that you swing inside to out across the target line. The ball will start to the right and then, in response to the left-to-right sidespin imparted by the brushing action of the square-to-target club face, it will curve back on target. There, again as simply as possible, is your draw.

Golfers with faulty shot patterns already deeply ingrained in their games may need to use this kind of alignment adjustment to reduce the curve of their shots to manageable proportions as a prelude to building a better swing.

For example, if you are a wild slicer—that is, you now curve many of your long shots way to the right in a vicious version of the fade—then you may need, for a time, to align your feet and shoulders a little closed (aimed to the right) of the target at address. This will quickly reduce your stubborn tendency to hit the ball with the club head traveling across the target line from the outside—*so long as you swing along the line parallel to your shoulders,* not *the direct target line.* With intelligent practice, this simple setup and swing-path adjustment will not only change your wild slice into a gentle draw, but will also eliminate

ALTER STANCE TO CURE RADICAL SHOT PATTERNS

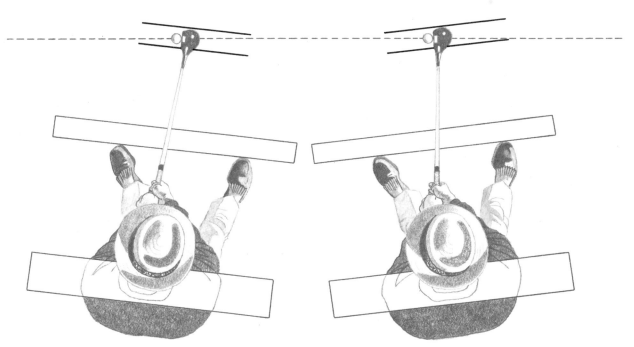

A square alignment of shoulders and feet to the target line may not be the ticket for those golfers who have already grooved a bad shot pattern. If you're a confirmed slicer, try standing with your feet and shoulders closed to the target line (left). If you hook the ball all the time, try standing more open to the line (right). In each case, make sure you swing along your natural club-head path and not along the target line. Such adjustments in stance should help you to gradually tame a too-severe shot pattern without forcing you to totally rebuild your swing.

from your game the slice-related faults of pulling, topping, hitting thin, and popping the ball weakly into the air.

Conversely, if you are that much rarer animal among handicap golfers, a congenital hooker—and understand that a hook is a shot that starts right of target before curving way left—then you need, for a time, to align your feet and shoulders a little *open* (aimed to the left) of the target at address. This will quickly reduce your tendency to hit the ball with the club head traveling across the target line too much from the inside—*again so long as you swing along the line parallel to your shoulders, not the direct target line.* And, as your hook turns into a fade, you'll find that your tendency to push shots and hit them fat will also diminish.

However, use these address-alignment adjustments carefully and intelligently. I've found in teaching that you often have to make a golfer who's sliced all his life actually hook the ball before he can grasp what's needed to fly it more or less straight. And, vice versa, that a vicious hooker needs to "feel" some wild slices before he can find the balance represented by the comparatively straight shot.

But the square stance should be the ultimate goal for all golfers in the long run, simply because it is the most natural from which to swing the club head squarely through the ball at maximum speed—which, in a nutshell, is all that golf consists of.

7: How to Build Your Grip and Stance into Your Shot-Making Procedure

LET'S start out here by placing the foundations of grip and stance in the framework of actual shot making, which I think will help us avoid a lot of unnecessary procedural problems later on. In golf, perhaps more than in most other sports, there is a need for a kind of Standard Operating Procedure in the way you approach the moment of execution. So, from the time you begin to groove a swing, you should also start grooving your pattern of approaching all shots.

Stepping up and hitting a golf ball well, during play or practice, is a complicated process done simply. Here, for example, is what a good golfer actually thinks and does, in a minute of time or less, prior to taking the club back on a normal shot.

The player:

Visualizes the shot (identifies its target and mentally plots its flight pattern).

Selects the club (decides on the weapon that will achieve the shot he "sees").

Eases the body (through deep breathing or light exercises, or whatever works best for the individual).

Steadies the mind (via entire ritual of shot preparation, including drawing on glove, teeing up ball, forming grip, and so on).

Steps into the shot (begins the address process).

Positions the body (adopts the posture most conducive to a full, free, yet carefully programmed swing).

Aligns the lower body (steps into the stance with both feet comfortably spaced at "comfortable" right angles to the target line, and a line across the toes pointing either slightly open, square, or closed, depending on the size and/or shape of the shot).

Aims the club (sets the club head behind the ball so that the bottom edge is at a right angle to an imaginary straight line from ball to target).

Positions the club (arranges it as it will be at impact in relation to body and ball).

Eases the body again (by waggling or simply lifting the club head from its static position behind the ball).

Aligns the upper body (by checking that the shoulder axis parallels the foot axis).

Visualizes the shot again (refocuses the mind on the intended behavior of the ball).

Makes the forward press, and begins the swing.

Seems like there's an awful lot involved, of course, when you analyze preparing for a shot as though it were the Normandy invasion. In fact, none of it is hard to understand or to accomplish, once you know exactly what you're trying to achieve and have habitualized the moves with a little practice.

The entire process actually involves only three major functions or activities:

1. Getting yourself relaxed and attentive, which is largely mental.

2. Setting yourself and your club correctly to ball and target, which is a question of aim.

3. Letting yourself begin the swing in one fluid motion, which comes from employing the most underrated device in the game—the forward press.

THE MENTAL CHALLENGE

Let's examine the mental challenge first.

To free yourself to swing effectively, you must develop a businesslike and orderly approach to each shot, and a level of concentration that keeps outside distractions or mental fuzziness from taking your mind off the job at hand. Such an approach allows you to make decisions with confidence about what club you're going to use and what shot you're going to play even before you get to the ball. It amounts to a personal system for ordering the variables in the shot situation—"personal" because, to a certain extent, only you can decide how to organize your approach to best suit your makeup.

Some variables—what club to use and where to aim—apply on every shot. Others depend on circumstances: the effects of wind or unusual fairway conditions; the adjustments in stance required by ususual lies; if you're playing a match, the present competitive situation (playing safe vs. gambling); and so on.

Seemingly trivial activities connected with shot preparation can distract you if they are not handled properly. Take, for instance, the simple chore of teeing up the ball. For all normal tee shots, I plug the wooden peg into the ground down to a depth where I can feel the grass on my knuckles, and no farther. (I actually hold my first two fingers under the ball in the usual manner, pressing palm downward on the ball to drive the peg in.) That ensures that my ball will be sitting at the same height for all my tee shots: I systematized that detail years ago and have never

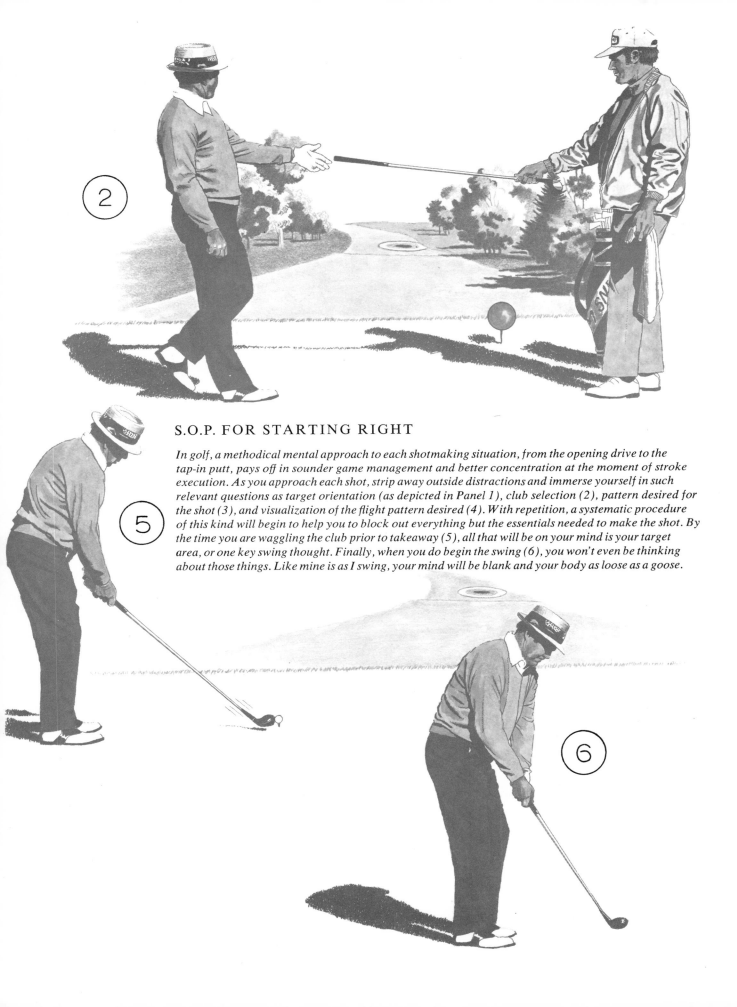

S.O.P. FOR STARTING RIGHT

In golf, a methodical mental approach to each shotmaking situation, from the opening drive to the tap-in putt, pays off in sounder game management and better concentration at the moment of stroke execution. As you approach each shot, strip away outside distractions and immerse yourself in such relevant questions as target orientation (as depicted in Panel 1), club selection (2), pattern desired for the shot (3), and visualization of the flight pattern desired (4). With repetition, a systematic procedure of this kind will begin to help you to block out everything but the essentials needed to make the shot. By the time you are waggling the club prior to takeaway (5), all that will be on your mind is your target area, or one key swing thought. Finally, when you do begin the swing (6), you won't even be thinking about those things. Like mine is as I swing, your mind will be blank and your body as loose as a goose.

had to think about it, much less worry over it, since. Yet I've played with golfers who actually tee up the ball at different heights on every hole without even knowing they do so. They haven't learned to systematize that particular simple detail of the game, and as a result they give themselves an unnecessary variable to adjust to every time they hit a drive.

So many of the golfers I've run across step up to the ball in a frazzled state because they let procedural details overpower their concentration. They tug their golf glove on at the last second, or they grope around for a tee, or they fail to realize it's their turn to hit until the last moment. The overall disruptive effect of these distractions on a golfer's composure can be monumental, and resulting shots are almost always misconceived or rushed.

Your goal should be to make the basic shot-making decisions early, clearly, and firmly, and then to ritualize all the necessary acts of preparation. Each act thus incorporated will then actually heighten concentration, not lessen it.

AIM

Aiming yourself and your club takes place in the course of assuming grip and stance.

There's a psychological dimension to the mechanical goal of aiming correctly. Mechanically, you strive to set up so that you are in a position to hit the ball squarely and directly toward the target. Psychologically, correct alignment is necessary to pacify the devils of doubt and uncertainty ready to spring up from your subconscious at the slightest provocation. If you don't line up so that you are going to hit the ball very close to the bottom of the downswing, or so that the club is going to meet the ball traveling momentarily on a line that leads directly to your target, then you will unconsciously compensate for the error by making adjustments in your swing.

If, for instance, you have positioned the ball too far back in your stance, your tendency when you swing will be to inhibit the forward thrust of your legs, in order for the club head to hit the back rather than the top of the ball, which in turn will encourage you to uncock your wrists too soon. Or, if you have aimed too far to the right of your target at address, your tendency as you start down will be to throw the club forward with your shoulders and/or hands in an instinctive effort to get it back in line.

Actually, it is possible to make late, split-second compensations for aiming mistakes and save the shot, but generally any compensatory move simply compounds the error, even for the pro. Worse, if the inept golfer is not aware of the responsiveness of the subconscious to his aiming mistakes, there is a big danger that his misunderstanding of the cause of missed shots will lead, through endless experiment, to total confusion about his technique.

If you finish wrapping your hands around the handle of the club before soling the club, no matter how stylistically correct your grip may be, it is possible that you will then set the club face behind the ball off line—looking either to the left or to the right of target. So make sure that you sole the club flat on the ground before completing the assembly of your hands on the club. And then, after you've gripped, and set the club behind the ball, check to see that the club has remained properly soled and that it is correctly aimed, with its leading edge at right angles to the imaginary straight line running from ball to target.

After the club is gripped and set to the ball, the next step in relating accurately to the target line, and thus completing your aiming procedure, is to assume your stance.

In setting the body to the ball, the idea is always to put the club in the same position at address that it should occupy at the moment of impact. For the driver, this means stepping into your stance so the ball is positioned directly opposite your left heel. As the clubs shorten, the ball is gradually positioned farther back until, with the five iron and all shorter clubs, it is opposite a point midway between your feet.

At all times, if your hands at address are to be where they should be at impact, they'll be *ahead* of the club face. How much ahead? Simply let the club sole flat on the ground and it will automatically place your hands as far ahead of the ball as they should be, relative to the length and loft of the club.

Since you are positioning the ball in your stance in relation to your left foot, that's the foot to finally position first as you assemble and adjust your stance. Once the left foot is correctly positioned, you simply draw the right foot in comfortably according to our stance-building rules—an inch or two farther back from the target line for the driver, in my case, and no farther away from your left foot than your right shoulder is from your left shoulder.

Understand that, in assembling a stance, you just don't clunk down one foot and then clunk down the other, and there it is. Once you've taken those basic alignment steps, there will always be some slight adjustments to make by wiggling and sliding your feet around, in order to get yourself relaxed and comfortably positioned over the ball.

Since it's very common for golfers to line up accurately in their feet and legs, but misalign their hips and shoulders, it is also useful to build into the setup procedure a means of checking that the upper and lower body alignments match each other. If I am standing correctly to the ball, a line through my shoulders parallels a line across my toes. When these two lines are parallel—when I feel that my shoulder axis and the line across my toes are identical—then I know that my upper body is aligned to the same target as my lower body, and I'm confident about swinging the club.

At this late point in setting up to the shot, it pays to bring your mind to bear on the target as intently as you know how. Try to project the shot you want to make on your mind's radar screen. As you look down your intended line, revisualize the picture you made prior to stepping up to the ball, when you first decided on the shot and target area and picked out the right club for the job. Only this time, get the picture into crystal-clear focus. If you've systematically prepared yourself for the shot up to now, there are no distractions left, no last-second doubts or indecisions to baffle you, and you can really pour on that concentration.

Now you're almost ready to swing. After your final orientation of mind and body to target, you set the club head behind the ball again. Your eyes shift from the target to the relationship before you of hands, club, and ball, which is almost exactly the relationship you want at impact. *That's your last visual image before takeoff.*

Note that I'm not recommending that you merely keep your eye on the ball, but that you also observe the ball in the correct relationship to your club and your hands. You'll find this a far more purposeful form of concentration than simply staring at the golf ball until it begins to hypnotize you.

8: The Forward Press—Golf's Most Underrated Move

EVEN the most methodical S.O.P. for starting right won't get your shot off the ground if you succumb to nervousness or tension in the course of preparing to swing.

There are several techniques for staying "loose as a goose" before every shot.

Simple exercises will relieve any tension you notice building up in your body in the course of a round or practice session. A couple of shallow knee bends, for instance, are a great help when your legs begin to feel stiff or "tight" or tired. Stretching your arms out in front of you to shoulder height will similarly free up tense shoulder muscles, and taking a few deep breaths calms you down generally. You'll see me doing all these things in the course of any tournament round.

Making a practice swing helps many golfers collect their energies and concentration for the shot. These days I seldom make one, except when the game is delayed for some reason while I'm waiting at the ball, or when I am feeling really tense. It's a matter of personal need or preference. I would only say that golfers should make sure they don't use the practice swing as a stalling device, when they should be deciding on their shot instead of practicing their swing. There's also the danger of exerting yourself so completely during a practice swing that you are actually less attentive and physically alert for the swing that counts.

As they settle their feet into the stance, many good golfers also give the club head a waggle, to prevent the hands and arms from tensing up. Waggling really amounts to no more than playing with the weight of the club head—sensing it by moving it around slightly.

I don't recommend an elaborate waggle, however. I think simply lifting the club head off the ground briefly, at the point in your setup when you're checking target alignment for the last time, and then replacing it behind the ball, is about all the waggle you really require. If the waggle is too long and drawn out, it may impede rather than encourage a smooth takeaway.

For my money, the single most important device for getting nerves and muscles ready to execute the golf swing properly is the forward press.

I've never made a golf swing that did not start from a forward press, and I've never met a golfer who failed to play better after learning to trigger his swing this way.

It's a very simple move. All that happens is that both hands press the club very slightly toward the target, while the right knee simultaneously inclines slightly toward the ball. Both moves cause weight to shift a little to the left, toward the target. As the weight shifts back, the takeaway begins, almost as a reflex or rebound action.

These movements may seem very slight or very pronounced, depending on the golfer, but properly done they accomplish two things.

First, they free the golfer's body from the pressures that have been accumulating in the setup, in spite of waggling and such. I've stressed the need to keep the approach to the ball as simple and uncluttered as possible. For all that, it is well-nigh humanly impossible to finally ad-

FORWARD PRESS STARTS
EVERYTHING BACK TOGETHE

The forward press takes many forms in golf, some much more noticeable than others, but in all cases th golfer exerts some slight physical pressure more or less in the direction of his target prior to swinging. This pressure may be as simple and nearly impercep ble as a slight weight shift toward the target, or as obvious as pressing on the handle of the club so firml that the shaft bends a bit. A forward press of some kind is desirable because it dissipates nervous tensio and permits the muscles to operate in unison in takin the club back from the ball.

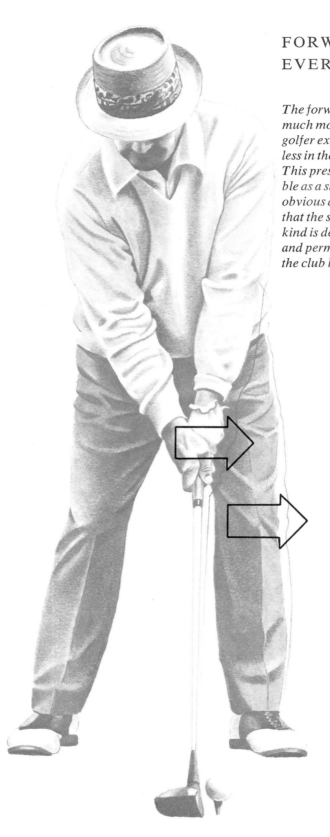

dress a golf ball without having collected some kind of tension in your body, because what you have been doing is finding and then occupying the correct *static* position from which to swing. Now you must set the body free to move through a series of *dynamic* positions. The forward press smooths the transition from static to dynamic better than anything else I've ever come across in a lot of years of searching.

The second blessing of the forward press is the help it gives you in starting back in one piece—with a unified action. Coordinating the action of the hands as they move the club back with the turning of the rest of the body is extremely difficult from a dead stop. Golfers without a forward press start the backswing sometimes with the hands, sometimes with the knees, sometimes with the feet, sometimes with the shoulders or head, and then wonder why they have such a hard time building and maintaining a consistent swing. The forward press eliminates that kind of initial jerkiness, by stimulating in one small action all the nerves and muscles used in golf, and thereby allowing the full swing to be initiated as a *reactive* movement, rather than in cold blood.

Although the action of the press may seem slight in some tour golfers, it must always be positive and never tentative. That's why I tell golfers who are still in the process of grooving their swings to at first make the press so firm that they can see the shaft of the club bend a bit. Later on, most players do not need to apply that much pressure. But it really is up to the individual, finally, to decide just how pronounced an action he needs to take to get his swing triggered smoothly.

The forward press—nothing more than a large, flowing swing springing from a small pressing action—originated way back in the mists of Scotland, but its underlying role is actually not unique to golf. It exists, in many guises, as a "trigger" in various activities and sports. For example, when you push yourself away from a desk, before getting up, you are executing a kind of forward press. The tennis player who rocks slightly toward his opponent, before rocking back into his service windup, is making another kind of forward press. So is the diver who pushes downward on the board slightly before thrusting his body into the air.

There is thus nothing old fashioned or artificial about a good forward press. It is a natural and vital part of your starting procedure. It helps keep a young swing fluid and an old swing young.

Part III
THE SWING
IN ACTION

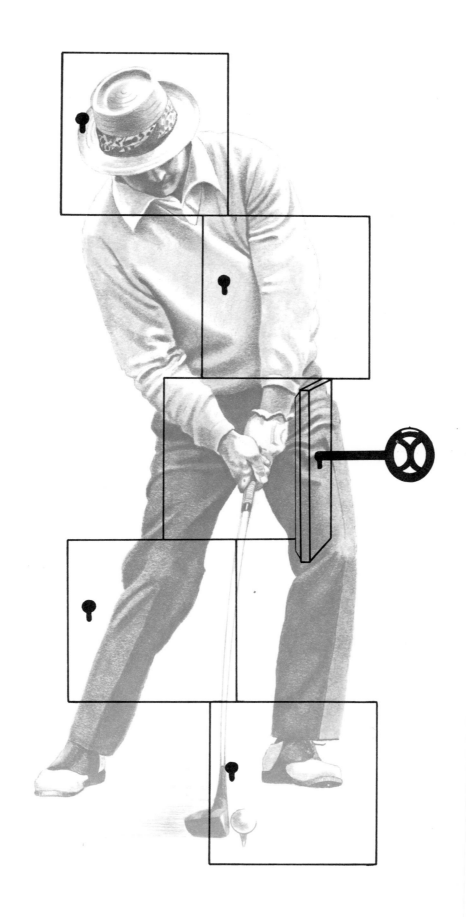

9: The "Key" Approach — How to Make It Work for You

EVERY year one pro or another will go on a winning binge on tour that gets everybody's attention. To the public it looks like a miracle, but in fact playing sharp as a tack for a time is never the result of magic. What happens is that particular abilities and experiences built up over the years emerge at the same time and in just the right mix to make for a spell of peak performances.

Tour golfers on hot streaks will seldom give the press a single reason for what they're doing, the main reason being that there isn't one. Another factor is that they don't particularly want to think about what's happening, let alone talk about it. They just want to hang on and ride it out for as long as it will last. That's why these players generally appear so cool and detached at such times. They're on automatic pilot— and that part *is* a little magical.

If a pro is thinking at all when he catches fire, it's usually only about one little thing—some word or picture or simple concept that in reality can't possibly account for the complex variety of shots that are behind his winning score. But, in the shorthand of his mind and body for that period of time, that word or picture or simple concept captures the total working order of the fellow's swing. It says it all.

I call that a "key"—a fundamental applied in the context of an actual swing. That's the basis of how I built my swing in the first place, and how I've managed to coax it to stay on track all these years. And that is the basis on which I'm writing this book.

In golf, thinking and doing have to be merged in such a way that each one helps, rather than hinders, the other. Through the use of swing keys that are easy to understand, feel, and apply, you can achieve a unity of thinking and doing that will keep your technique in good running order season after season.

What the keys do is simplify your understanding of the golf swing so that, when you step up to the ball, you can blank out all the garbage and concentrate with total intensity on executing the shot you've planned.

What's the difference between a "key" and a "gimmick," say, or a "cure"?

I would say that a key, since it must affect the total swing, is born of proven fundamentals closely related to basic swing objectives. For instance, "Keep your left arm straight" is not really a key, because it is an isolated command out of the context of the dynamics of the swing. A more fundamental approach, and one that would influence the swing in its entirety, would urge, "Keep elbows together throughout the swing." That is a key to good arm action because it not only firms up the left arm—which is pretty good advice for most golfers—but it also keeps both arms working together as a unit throughout the entire motion of the swing, which is fundamental to striking a golf ball effectively.

78

Think of the golf swing, for a moment, as one of those elaborate locking systems used on bank vaults. Within the vault, tumblers and bars and wheels and such interact in a complicated way—to keep my prize money safe. A bank official can open the vault simply by dialing the correct combination, which trips a mechanism that sets the various tumblers and bars and wheels working together to make the vault open with a "click." To me, the components of that vault's locking system are analogous to the various actions and reactions of the different parts of the body during the golf swing. The tripping mechanism is analogous to the kind of key I am talking about, in the way I learned golf as a kid, and in the way I play and teach it today.

A key is simple and confined to one particular element or phase of swing action, yet it prompts an elaborate sequence of actions that result in hitting the golf ball with a "click" and not a "clunk."

SELECTION OF THE KEYS

In the next few chapters you will learn exactly how to swing the club through the use of specific keys related to the action of the hands, posture, and body movement; and, through some tips on timing, how to correctly blend those hand actions and body movements.

Although the keys are presented in separate groups, your prime objective in selecting keys to apply to your own game will be to properly correlate the hand action to the body movement. Too often golfers work on one at the expense of the other. They start working on their "leg action" or their "shoulder turn," and before long the hands are coming apart at the top, or the hands are delivering the club head to the ball too late. Or golfers devote themselves so exclusively to holding the club with the proper grip that the rest of the body falls asleep.

Combining one hand key and one body key is the surest way I know to avoid this kind of problem, because it helps you to attack your swing from two different but equally important angles. For example, if you've been having trouble "hitting from the top," thinking in terms of attaining the "power slot" position at the top (a hand key), and thrusting your right knee forward at the start of the downswing (a body key), should improve your performance right away.

Also, in using this book be prepared to select keys according to your *sense*—your intuitive feeling—about what is lacking or malfunctioning in your present swing. For example, if you are generally aware that your hand position at the top varies from swing to swing, or that there is a lack of any significant lower body action in your downswing, study the hand key related to the power slot, or pick a body key to get your feet or knees moving.

Let me warn right away that golfers will respond in different ways to the suggestions contained in the various keys. That is why some keys will work for one golfer and others will not, and why, ultimately, it is up to the individual to be intelligently selective about the keys, based on the results of practice.

Let me also warn that not all hand and body keys will ever be relevant to your swing at any one time, if only because it would be impossible to execute a swing with all the keys in mind. I want to stress that point, since earlier I made a lot of fuss about the need for simplicity in the golf swing. I still believe that, so be ready to limit your own efforts to no more than two or three keys at a time.

Many different combinations of keys may be put together, as you will see. In fact, you will almost certainly have to try a number of combinations before you happen on those that dramatically improve your swing.

And be prepared for a key—whether it's a hand key or body key—suddenly to become at least temporarily ineffective in your game. It may cease to work for you simply because you've used it so long that you have involuntarily exaggerated it. Or it may have become inappropriate to the particular problem you're presently experiencing in your swing. In such cases, the key will not be able to stimulate a positive result, so it is time to "retire" it temporarily. Don't let that worry you, because some day it will be useful to you again. But, for now, be ready to try something else.

PRACTICING THE KEYS

Hand and body keys are presented with the full swing in mind. In preparing to groove this swing, which is your ultimate goal, it is best to build from the core of the swing outward—that is, from the more manageable actions and movements of shorter strokes first.

The best way to start familiarizing yourself with the hand keys is by practicing short shots with a well-lofted, short-shafted, easy-to-hit club like the nine iron or pitching wedge. In fact, ambitious golfers of every caliber would benefit handsomely by setting up a small "chipping range" in their back yard or basement. All it takes is a small basket or pail to serve as the target, a couple of dozen old golf balls, and perhaps a piece of carpet or mat to serve as the fairway. Spend a few minutes a day chipping with a nine iron or wedge and you'll be surprised how much "feel" you develop for making accurate short shots that depend entirely on good timing and the loft of the club. And how clearly you will come to sense—to "feel"—the moves inherent in the keys, especially the hand keys.

I can't stress too much the need to develop this kind of feel for the benefit of your entire golf game, not just your use of the hand keys. It builds a sense of the kind of flush contact between club face and ball that you are striving for on all shots, from the full drive to the shortest putt, and it teaches you, in miniature form, all the actions intrinsic to the full swing. Those are its general values. Its direct and immediate value is that you develop confidence in those little shots around the green that depend almost entirely on touch. And, even after you have

81

developed an effective golf swing, this is a phase of the game to which you must devote a lot of regular practice if you ever want to score really well.

Body keys can be developed first by practicing with a five iron, and then working your way up to the wood clubs. The five iron is the ideal practice club because it has enough loft to get the ball in the air fairly easily, and yet its shaft is long enough to require a substantial body turn and weight shift. Swinging with too long or lightly lofted a club can be discouraging when you first attempt to build a swing or cope with changing your existing swing.

Full-swing practice can be overdone, by the way. Hackers consistently make the mistake of beating hundreds of balls on a practice range with either nothing or too much in mind. Quantity does not make up for lack of quality. So try to practice to a fine point with a key or two in mind, then quit when you're ahead. If you keep on to the point of either mental or physical fatigue, you'll lose your edge. A lot of the youngsters on tour have yet to learn this simple lesson.

Working on your golf swing through hand, body, and timing keys is a lifelong endeavor. Your emphasis on individual keys and combinations of keys will continue to change as you try to keep up with the latest quirks or weaknesses in your game and your metabolic and mental condition. Even a good golf swing is always on the brink of chaos, because it is such a subtle combination of physical moves and mental discipline. Like any high-precision instrument, the tendency of the swing is always to go out of tune. Finding and using workable keys is the secret to keeping the swing in tune and on track.

10: Hand Keys: Know Your "Action Positions"

YOU can play a reasonable form of golf without the benefit of sight, say, or the use of your legs—blind and handicapped persons have proven that. But stick your hands in your pockets and you might as well find a new game. The complicated action of the golf swing just could not be performed without the amazing dexterity of human hands. The hands channel strength and speed on every swing, and greatly influence the shape and direction of every shot.

When I observed, in first learning the game, that my hands were really my only connection with the golf club, I realized I would have to find out exactly what those hands had to do at every significant point in the swing. My study of the key action positions of the hands, which I'm now going to describe in detail, has always—in conjunction with my keys to body movement and timing—formed the basis for my work with pupils, and for my on-going scrutiny of my own swing. Whenever something feels out of whack in my swing or my shots start going haywire, I first check my hands in terms of the key action positions, detailed below, to locate the problem.

I'd like to suggest you use this chapter on hand keys in a similar manner, namely: (1) to build your awareness of what your hands are doing during the swing, and (2) to correct and improve the action positions that, in your present swing, feel sloppy or unproductive.

Don't forget—you have to walk before you can run. I repeat that the worst way to get acquainted with your hand action is by using your driver, and that the best way is by chipping short shots with a well-lofted club, and then *gradually* moving into the full swing with the longer clubs.

HAND KEY 1: GRIP PRESSURE— KEEP IT LIGHT, BUT NOT LOOSE

As I pointed out in the earlier chapter on the grip, pressure is applied in a good golf grip to specific points along the club handle rather than uniformly. That's because uniform pressure throughout the hands does not permit the springy, resilient control over the club, plus the wrist flexibility, that is needed during the full golf swing.

In terms of the broad application of hand pressure, there should be relatively *little*. Sure, the club must be held fairly firmly in order to secure it in the hands for the duration of the swing. But don't squeeze the sawdust out of the shaft, as so many hackers do. What you want to achieve is the kind of light feeling in your fingers that you have when you throw a stick for a dog to fetch.

Make sure that you never hold the club so tightly that your forearms begin to tighten up on you as you address the ball. A tight grip keeps the wrist from working properly later on, and actually encourages the hands to come apart, not, as one might think, to stay together as they must, especially at the top of the backswing and start of the downswing.

84

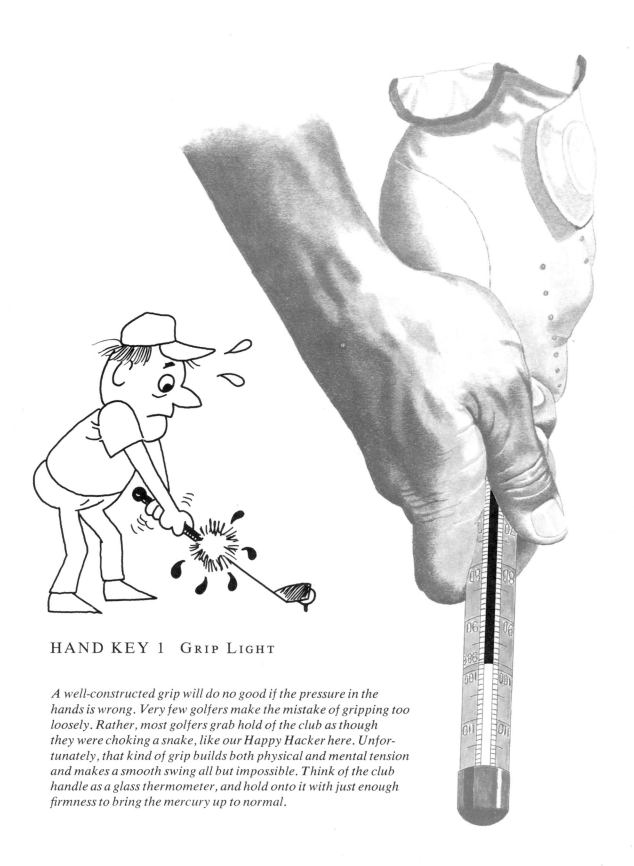

HAND KEY 1 GRIP LIGHT

A well-constructed grip will do no good if the pressure in the hands is wrong. Very few golfers make the mistake of gripping too loosely. Rather, most golfers grab hold of the club as though they were choking a snake, like our Happy Hacker here. Unfortunately, that kind of grip builds both physical and mental tension and makes a smooth swing all but impossible. Think of the club handle as a glass thermometer, and hold onto it with just enough firmness to bring the mercury up to normal.

Holding the club more in the fingers than in the palms is the key to a light grip for generating maximum club-head speed with control. In this respect, the baseball pitcher's wrist action is close to the good golfer's action. You'd get no speed with a baseball if you held it in your palm, because you'd get no wrist snap, no elasticity. Same way in golf. Hold the club in your palms and you'll feel strongly in control of it, but you'll get no wrist snap. In golf you *must* have wrist snap, and, if you can get it right, you'll knock the ball a mile. Wrist action is your supercharger. Never forget that.

Is there any difference in firmness between the pressure points of the two hands? I would say that most good golfers hold on a little bit more with the boxing-in action of the two last fingers and butt of the left hand than they do with the pinching pressure of the thumb and forefinger of the right hand. My own sense of pressure at the beginning of the swing is that the right hand holds sway briefly during the forward press, but that, as the takeaway begins, the pressure of the left hand increases, smoothly and sufficiently to make sure that the club moves back in a slow, low, full arc. This slightly greater grip pressure in my left hand also helps to prevent my right hand from picking the club up too quickly on the way back—a fault of 90 percent of middle- and high-handicap golfers.

HAND KEY 2: ADDRESS BALL WITH HANDS IN THE ''HOLSTER''

We've seen how an unbalanced grip forces a golfer to make unnecessary compensations in the way he swings the club. An improper action position of the hands at address causes similar problems. Understand that the hands must be placed correctly, both on the club and in relation to your body and the ball, in order for you to swing the club back easily to your best possible hitting position at the top.

86

For all normal shots, the hands should be positioned just far enough away from the body for the arms to swing the club *freely* back and *freely* through past the body. But, as I mentioned in an earlier chapter, I've very rarely seen a golfer whose hands were set too close to his body at address. Rather, most golfers tend to reach for the ball, extending their arms forward rather than letting them hang down. That upsets their natural balance by pulling their weight forward, flattens the plane of the swing more than necessary, and generally disturbs tempo and reduces power and control.

When I address the ball with the driver, the butt end of the club is a few inches from the inside of my forward leg. That proximity puts me in position to make a smooth, upright, balanced swing and to maintain full control over the club with my hands throughout the action.

A good way to make sure that you're not reaching for the ball at address is to make a "false swing"—bring your hands up and then back down again without disturbing your balance. If you're reaching, the club face will return to the impact position too much on the near side of the ball.

A second common mistake among poorer golfers is varying the hand position at address in relation to the ball. For some shots they set their hands even with the ball, for others ahead of or behind the ball. Here is another variable that no one needs. For *every* club in the bag (except possibly the putter), your hands should be set slightly ahead of the ball at address, opposite the inside of your forward leg, and as close to your body as possible without inhibiting the making of a full and comfortable arm swing. That is your key hand position at the start of the swing.

For all normal shots, and with every club in the bag, you can actually think—as I do—of the hands at address being in their proper action position when they're in an imaginary holster directly off the inside of your forward leg. If you put your hands in the "holster" prior to each and every shot, you'll be starting your gunfights with your best

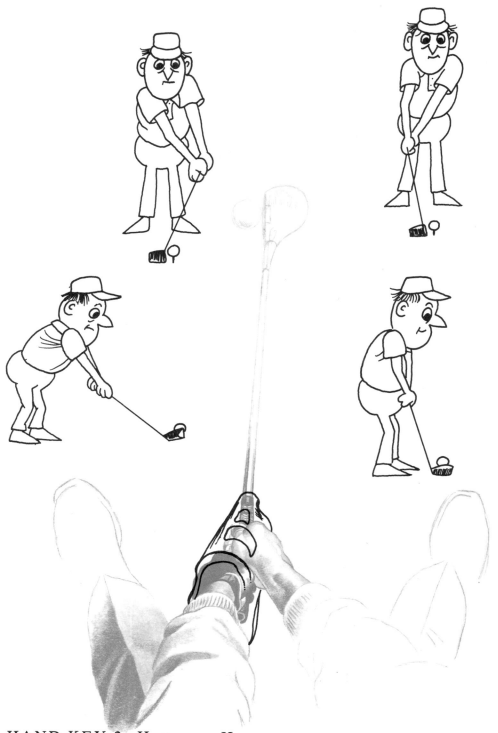

HAND KEY 2 HANDS IN HOLSTER

One of the most common variables that club golfers introduce into their games to no good purpose is the position of the hands in relation to ball and body at address. For all normal shots with any club in the bag (except the putter), the hands should be placed at almost exactly the same position off the forward thigh, in a kind of imaginary holster that never is shifted up or down or left or right. Of all the incorrect positions of the hands at address illustrated here by the Happy Hacker, the most common is standing too far away from the ball.

chance of shooting far and true.

Let's put this holster concept another way. The position of the ball in your stance changes only according to the length and angle of the shaft of the club you have selected to do the job. But once you've got your "holster," your hand position within that stance *does not change;* your hands are always in the same place. For the long-shafted driver, when the club is flatly soled behind the ball and the hands are set in the holster position, the ball emerges forward in the stance, about opposite the inside of the forward heel. As the clubs decrease in shaft length and increase in loft, the ball naturally positions itself farther back in the stance until, with the five iron, it is opposite a point about midway between your feet. Yet, for driver or five iron, your hands are in exactly the same holster.

The most important role of a good action position of the hands at address is to present to your eye the correct picture of impact, and to impart to your muscles' memory the preferred impact configuration of club, body, and ball. It's always easier to swing to a position you have occupied than to swing to a new one. That is why you should concentrate on setting up at address in a posture that mirrors the most desirable impact position.

This is always the final image to have in your mind as you begin to swing: hands are ahead of the ball; the club face is looking directly at the target; the body is lithe, resilient, and in balance; and there, before you, is the exact relationship of hands, club, and ball that you aim to reproduce at the bottom of your downswing.

HAND KEY 3: LEFT HAND CREATES TAKEAWAY ARC

The initial extension of the club away from the ball determines the overall speed, smoothness, and shape of the swing. It may help you to

HAND KEY 3 LEFT HAND CREATES TAKEAWAY ARC

Control of the initial phases of the backswing should be firmly in the left hand, to ensure that the club is drawn back as smoothly and in as full an arc as possible. The Happy Hacker demonstrates the most common failing among average golfers, picking the club up with an overactive right hand, and the less common fault of forcing the club face to remain unnaturally "square" to the target. Study my hands for the correct pattern of backswing hand action and alignment.

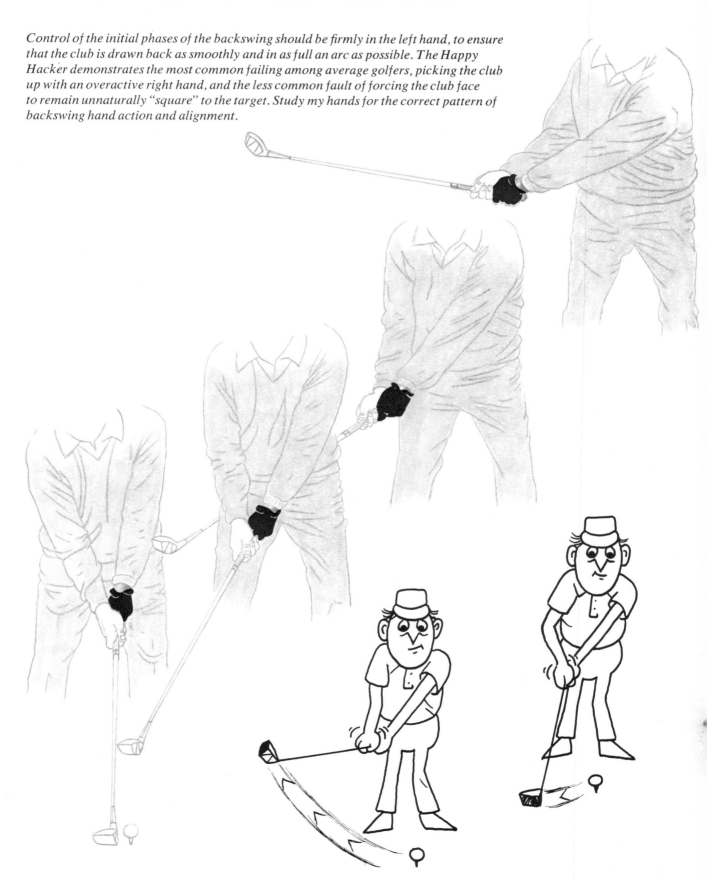

know that I take the driver back with as much care, in terms of keeping it square to my target, for the first foot or so of its journey as I use in taking a putter back from the ball on the green.

The club should be drawn away from the ball, smoothly and low to the ground, and as far back along the ground as you can extend it away from you without pulling your head off center.

As (or immediately after) the forward press is executed, control of the club should pass to the left hand. It is the left hand that governs and is the key to the takeaway-action position I've just described.

The left hand tends to *direct* the club for a foot or so along a line running directly back from the ball, and to do that it must be in control as the swing starts. If, instead, the right hand *pulls* or lifts the club back, there will be a great risk of it moving abruptly either to the inside or outside of the line, and of the wrists cocking too soon. Almost every golfer's right hand wants to disrupt and hurry the action at this point. But it must be controlled if the maximum swing arc is to be created and a smooth takeaway motion is to be grooved—the only way to repeatability.

Think of your left hand acting simply as a carrier for the club at this point, with no independent life of its own. It simply links the arm and the club in a straight line as the club starts back, and these parts continue to form a straight line during the takeaway for as long as possible.

The pushing action of the left hand naturally pulls the left shoulder around the head, which is the fixed center point, or axis, of the body pivot, and the left knee also begins to be pulled inward toward the ball. Thus, the takeaway can be seen as the span in the swing when the entire left side is turned into action.

HAND KEY 4 WRISTS COCK WAIST HIGH

Happy shows the usual hand-action faults at this stage in the backswing, either cocking the wrists too soon, as though he were hoisting a shovel up on his shoulders, or not letting the wrists cock at all, and thus greatly diminishing the swing arc and thereby the power potential. If a smooth left-hand-controlled takeaway has been made, the wrists should begin to cock or hinge when the hands reach about waist high. And remember that the gathering momentum in the backswing and the weight of the club head at the other end of the shaft will encourage your wrists to cock naturally, without any conscious manipulation on your part.

HAND KEY 4: LET WRISTS COCK IN RESPONSE TO SWINGING CLUB HEAD

The left hand's "carrier" pushing action continues until the wrists of both hands begin to naturally hinge or cock, which should not be until the hands reach about waist high, after which the wrists continue hinging gradually until the hands reach the top of the swing.

The wrist cock is an integral part of the backswing, and should not be cultivated as an independent action.

My point is that the wrist cock should occur as a natural *reflex* action in response to the swinging weight of the club head, with no manipulation or stress involved. And such a reaction is all that is needed to deliver the club into a position from which it can strike the ball decisively.

Think, as I do, of slowly pulling the wrist cock out of your side pocket as your hands pass the level of your waist. *And let the wrists break the way that feels natural for them to break at that point.* Too much conscious thought about the mechanics or angles of wrist cocking tends to make a golfer start manipulating his hands in odd ways.

Experiment without a golf club to see exactly how your wrists should hinge as the backswing develops. Stick your left arm out in front of you and hold the fingers and thumb out straight. Then, without moving your forearm, bend the wrist to the left, to the right, and straight up. You'll probably find that it will bend to the left about 45 degrees, to the right about 80 degrees, and straight up only about 30 degrees.

In the golf swing, the wrists cock almost exclusively straight up, along the side of and in line with the forearm. For the right hand, it's akin to throwing a pass in football, rather than the wrist action involved, say, in knocking on a door.

The wrist cock appears to begin earlier in the backswing on short irons than on long clubs because the hands naturally react to the club head sooner when shaft length is reduced and head weight increases in proportion to total club weight. But, relative to your arm swing and body turn, the wrists cock at the same tempo and at the same point, which is as your hands pass about waist high. And, remember, they should always cock in response to the swinging weight of the club head, rather than in response to a conscious mental effort.

HAND KEY 5: AT THE TOP, SWING INTO YOUR POWER SLOT

The key action position of my hands at the top is what I call a "power slot," equidistant between the back of my head and the extremity of my right shoulder, with the hands *under* the club handle, the grip firmly intact, and the wrists cocked naturally and only to the degree demanded by the swinging weight of the club head.

The back of the left hand and the left arm here form a straight line —or as straight as you can manage according to your natural strength. Many golfers must bend the left hand forward slightly, so the wrist is a bit concave, in reaching for as full a turn as possible. As long as the bend is slight, the swing will not suffer. And it is better to have a little concave bend at the wrist than to create rigidity and tension by trying too consciously for a "straight" wrist position.

The ideal top-of-the-swing slot is a high hand position, showing there's a good deal of body windup (and thus leverage) built into it, and that's why I call it the power slot. The power is on the top shelf in golf, and you have to reach for it.

A good way to check your own power slot is to swing the club back to the top and then stop. Now bring your hands out in front of you at shoulder level, with your wrists still cocked. Your hands and club

94

shaft should be nearly vertical, not angled off severely to left or right.

If your hands and club shaft are tilted to your left, it means that you are letting your left arm or wrist collapse on the backswing and thus either reducing your arc or disrupting your plane, or both.

If your hands and club shaft are tilted more than a few degrees to the right, it means that you have "laid off" at the top—the lazy man's backswing that indicates an early "pickup" of the club by the hands and arms and a lack of body coiling that, jointly, also limit your power potential.

To correct a faulty power-slot position, simply assume the correct grip on the club in front of your body and cock your wrists so that the club shaft is vertical. Then swing your shoulders around with your left arm firmly extended until your back faces the target and the shaft of the club parallels your target line. Now your hands are in the power slot that's right for you. That's the position you should try to memorize and swing back to every time.

This test applies *no matter what your build or swing plane*. Whether your hands tend to occupy a hitting position near your head, in the more upright position common among taller golfers, or near your right shoulder, in the flatter position, your hands should set vertically in the test I've just described if, in fact, you are swinging back to the power slot most natural for you. If they do not, it means you are swinging too flat or too upright for your particular stature.

Bringing the club into the power slot is the final phase of the backswing. It stretches the left side of the body to its limit but without any shifting of the head and neck, which serve throughout as the axis of the arm swing and body pivot, and it puts the hands and club into the best possible position from which to make a swinging hit. When, through practice, you have grooved a good position at the top; practically all you'll have left to do to perfect your swing is to get your timing right.

LAYING OFF

CROSSING THE LINE

HAND KEY 5 "POWER SLOT" AT THE TOP

Think of swinging your hands up to a hitting position that is approximately midway between your head and shoulder, and "memorize" that as the power slot to which you want to bring your hands on every full shot. A good checkpoint for this vital hand position is to swing the club to the top (above) and then, instead of executing the downswing, bring your hands and club around in front of you (right), without changing your grip or the way your wrists are set. If the club is just about vertical, your hands at the top are correctly in the power slot that is natural for your particular physique. If the club angles severely to left or right (opposite page), you are not reaching your true power slot position at the top. You're either laying off from the target line (when the club points to your right) or crossing the target line (when the club points left), two faults which cost power, and force unnecessary swing compensations.

HAND KEY 6: STARTING DOWN, PULL WITH YOUR LEFT-HAND FINGERS

The last two fingers of the left hand pull down on the club handle to start the downswing. Those are the two fingers with which the shaft was initially "boxed" most firmly in the left hand, forming the most important of the three key pressure points in the action position of the hands in assembling the grip. Now that pressure point becomes the predominant force in the action position of the hands at the start of the downswing.

Let me stress here that it is very important to keep that sensation of pulling limited to the last two fingers of the left hand. Trying to pull down with the *entire* left hand at this point will make you tend to grab the club handle, which will throw the club out of its natural downswing arc, causing the wrists to uncock prematurely and the right side of the body to lunge forward.

The pulling-down action of the last two fingers of the left hand is also the action position that initiates the lower-body weight shift back toward the target.

It is frequently argued today that the weight shift itself is the initiator of the downswing, because many good players do consciously think in terms of starting down by driving their legs forward or by turning their hips back toward the target, and this has thus become the emphasis of much modern teaching theory.

The reason I prefer an action position of the hands as the main igniter of my downswing, rather than a body key, is that I find it easier to initiate any action with consistency and rhythm by using small muscles instead of large muscles. In my swing, the comparatively small-scale action of the two fingers pulling down best triggers the large-scale action of the weight shift.

98

HAND KEY 6 START DOWN WITH LEFT-HAND FINGERS

More golfers initiate the downswing incorrectly than commit any other single fault in golf. Almost invariably the cause of the fault is grabbing or throwing the club with the right hand (as the Happy Hacker demonstrates) instead of pulling it down with the left hand. When the right hand starts the downswing action, the shoulders move forward, the wrists uncock, and both club-head speed and square delivery are inhibited. The key thought of pulling down on the club with the last two fingers of the left hand helps prevent the right hand from assuming command and throwing the club from the top. It encourages the simultaneous thrust toward target of the left side, too, a vital action which is always inhibited when the right hand is trying to run the show.

At times, however—for example, when you have become lazy in your legs and hips—you may find it advisable to think in terms of starting the downswing with the large muscles of your lower body. We'll later look at some body keys that will help you with this approach. However, the risk in starting down thinking primarily of body motion is that you can easily develop all kinds of exaggerated, lurchy-jerky moves that can very quickly cut your timing to ribbons.

Thinking in terms of starting down with the arms—as is also often recommended in some modern instruction—can eventually cause problems, too. Often it encourages the hands to go dormant on the downswing. The golfer then almost always hits too late by failing to let the club head catch up with his hands by impact through a full uncocking of the wrists, with the result that the club head is dragged across the ball with the face open, causing a slice.

Thinking in terms of starting down with *both* hands almost invariably causes the right hand to assert itself too soon and too powerfully, usually in a forced grabbing and throwing action. This is by far the most common problem golfers have with this action position, and it costs untold losses in distance due to the premature release of the hands. The club is thrown from the top of the swing in a kind of casting motion, with the wrists uncocking way too soon, which causes the shoulders to be pulled forward, which in turn causes the club to be thrown down to the ball from beyond—outside—the target line.

Pulling down from the top with the last two fingers of the left hand can be seen as a kind of delaying action. It helps to keep that right hand from jumping in too soon, and it gives your legs and hips time to begin turning the body weight nice and smoothly in the direction of your target.

Remaining in good balance at the bottom of the swing is usually a sign that you have started down properly.

HAND KEY 7: DOWN AND THROUGH— RIGHT HAND POURS IT ON

At this point, the golf swing becomes a series of reflex actions upon which a lot of conscious thoughts aren't going to have much effect, at least not at the moment of execution. There is a kind of "snap, crackle, and pop" sequence—the *snap* of the wrists uncocking after the hands have brought the club down below waist level, in response to centrifugal force; the *crackle* of the lower body driving smoothly forward and then turning toward the target; and the *pop* at the moment of impact.

A good way to acquaint yourself with this fastest-moving, and therefore hardest-to-mentally-direct phase of the swing, is periodically to practice swinging with your eyes closed. This better than anything else I know will help you feel what your hands are doing through impact. In swinging "blindfolded," concentrate on the feeling of your hand action *through* the ball. In baseball, the good batter hits the ball just as it comes over the plate, not before or after, and that correlation of hands and hitting area is exactly what we're after in golf. In mechanical terms, it is achieved by the release or uncocking of the wrists to the point where, at impact, they are in the same angular relationship to the arms and club that they occupied at address.

The key action position at this point in time is thus a feeling of the right hand pouring on the speed in the hitting area. Understand—particularly all you golfers who've heard or read those warnings about "too much right hand"—that using the right hand can't throw the swing off course at this point, because by now the club is moving too fast for its trajectory to be altered. What fully releasing the right hand at this point can and does do is simply sustain the club-head speed that has been maximized by centrifugal force, and through that maximizes power. The right hand's "pouring on" action at this stage also helps to

HAND KEY 7   RIGHT HAND POURS IT ON

In the free swing productive of maximum club-head speed, the right hand instinctively becomes more active in the last split seconds of the downswing, literally pouring on its strength and helping to bring the club head around and into the ball squarely and with maximum speed. Many golfers are afraid to use their right hand because, consciously or unconsciously, they believe that it is already too powerful an influence in the swing. Happy shows what happens (top) when the right hand comes in too soon, and (bottom) when it never gets into the act at all.

square the club face as both hands strive to reoccupy the position they were in at address—the ideal impact position with the club face looking squarely at the target and the left arm and shaft forming a straight line from shoulder to ball.

The "pouring on" action of the right hand is so distinct a sensation in my swing that I feel like I'm making the club head *chase* the ball so fast right on through impact and out toward the target that it might almost catch up with it.

HAND KEY 8: RIGHT HAND ROLLS OVER FIRM LEFT HAND

Ideally, at the finish, your arms would be extended as high on the target side of the ball as they were at the top of your backswing. In actuality, though, many good golfers never reach a finish position that is an exact mirror image of the position at the top—a golfer with a high backswing often finishing somewhat low, and a golfer with a short backswing often finishing comparatively high.

Nevertheless, it should be your goal to strive to finish with your hands in what amounts to a mirror image of the position they occupied in your power slot. Picture the way a good bowler always completes his swing—with his right arm across his body and his hand flung high between head and shoulder. That's your ideal.

Poorer golfers don't have a follow-through to speak of because they have not generated the club-head momentum necessary to create one. For all practical purposes, they have finished swinging the moment the club hits the ball—they hit "at" the ball rather than "through" it. Top golfers achieve such great club-head speed by swinging through the ball that the momentum of the club just forces the hands to fly on up to a good, high finish without any particular effort to achieve that position.

103

HAND KEY 8 ROLL HANDS TO HIGH FINISH

If the right hand has been allowed to "slap" yardage into the shot at impact, the right arm will naturally extend out straight toward the target after impact. The left arm also will remain firm and extended at this point—note especially that the left wrist has not caved in from the force of striking the ball, indicative of good left-hand control through impact. The high finish (ghosted figure) is a natural consequence of this last action position in the swing, but is not in itself as meaningful a checkpoint as the one shown. Happy demonstrates two common finishes among poor golfers, at top the result of a collapsing left hand, and at bottom the "pushing" action that results from no right-hand release.

The actual key hand position in the later stages of the follow-through is the turning of the right hand over the left hand, but note that this occurs *only as a result of your pouring it on with the right hand in the prior action position*. Note also that the left wrist *does not buckle inward*—concavely—at the wrist as the right hand rolls over it, but simply turns over so its back faces the ground as the club reaches the maximum extension toward the target, then faces behind the golfer at the finish of the follow-through.

If you finish without the right hand crossing over the left, you are not speeding into the shot with the right hand at impact, and that means you're not getting as much distance on the shot as you deserve and need. Indeed, such a "blocking" tendency is something I see a lot of in pro-ams today, as a result of all the instructional stress on left-sidedness and ultra-delayed release of the wrists.

While we're on the subject of blocking, it might help if I reiterated here that the club head in every good swing does not travel *along* the target line at impact for any appreciable distance, but simply fleetingly coincides with that line as it describes an inside-to-inside arc. For the club head to travel naturally back inside the target line after impact, the hands must rotate counterclockwise (as opposed to bending targetward at the wrists, mind). Any time you try to prevent this happening—usually by trying to force the club head *along* the target line too long—you will lose club-head speed and thus distance by blocking your hand-wrist motion.

11: Keys to Posture and Body Action

IN this chapter I am going to describe the roles played by the various parts of the body—from head to foot—in the dynamics of the golf swing. Then I'm going to identify and explain the key sensations and activities associated with each. Before we start trying to define each of the individual actions and feelings involved, let me give you my sense of how the body moves in the swing in its entirety. Thus you will be better able to keep my array of body keys in proper perspective.

After making my forward press, I feel that I wind up my body, pause, and then unwind my body—and that, in a nutshell, is my sense of the golf swing. The principal physical action is a turning of the hips and shoulders—working in tandem—around a fixed point. In accounting for other parts of my body and their principal roles in relation to this action, I would say that I maintain my balance during the swing principally through good footwork and a steady head position, and that I maintain my control of the club through my arms and, of course, through the action positions of my hands, detailed earlier.

Likening the swing to the action of a coil spring is more accurate than any other single idea or image in conveying to me what the body basically does in striking a golf ball. The more fully a golfer can wind up his body, the more powerfully he can unwind it back into the shot. The more he can unwind while in balance and in control of his club, the more club-head speed he will then deliver to the ball, which means the farther it will fly.

That is perhaps the most obvious reason why I try to get golfers to coil their bodies as fully as they can—*within their natural limits*—during the backswing.

But there are two other good reasons for lengthening the swing arc by maximizing the turn. First, a longer swing arc is easier to operate within than a short arc, because it provides more time and opportunity for correcting errors in hand or body actions before the ball is struck. Second, a longer swing arc grows old more gracefully than a short one. In other words, it is harder to lengthen a short swing and remain in your groove than it is to shorten a long swing. As the muscles of golfers who began in the game with a big turn grow less supple with age, their basic swings remain unspoiled, even though their turn may gradually be reduced, and distance inevitably lost.

Remember, try to link body keys to hand keys whenever feasible. You can do this one way by linking keys that relate to sensations or activities occurring simultaneously—for example, the hand key of the holster position can be implemented at the same time as the body key of pinching your knees inward at address. You can do it another way by linking keys that suggest a cause-and-effect relationship—for example, the hand key of starting down with a pull of the last two fingers of the left hand works smoothly with the body key of turning the hips back toward the target on the downswing.

BODY KEY 1 STAND UP TO THE BALL IN "HALVES"

In good golfing posture, the knees are comfortably flexed, the posterior is set out a bit, and the golfer leans forward slightly from the waist, with his arms hanging comfortably down and forward. The Happy Hacker shows what happens when either the legs or upper body is not at the proper golfing angle.

BODY KEY 1: STAND UP TO
THE BALL IN "HALVES"

The components of the stance, which I covered earlier, relate mainly to the target line and to the positioning of the golf club in relation to the body. Posture falls more within the province of this chapter on body keys, because it is as much the product of feeling as it is of specific positioning. Posture might be called the overall attitude of your body as you finalize your stance and your setup to the ball.

The key to effective posture lies in developing the habit of standing up to the ball as though you were composed of two distinctly different parts—one part from the waist down, the other part from the waist up.

To set your lower body properly, simply flex your knees slightly, then shove your backside toward the rear a bit. You'll feel this action primarily in your lower back and hips. It is comparable in feeling to the action you would take if, without moving your feet, you started to sit down in a chair that was slightly farther away from you than you had anticipated.

To set your upper body, simply lean forward from the waist with a straight back so that, if you were not holding a club, your arms would dangle straight down and point at your toes. Make sure you don't hunch your back or drop your head as you lean forward.

These two actions create a posture that gives the appearance of being fairly erect and upright—of "standing tall." But, in fact, the actions set each of the "parts" at a distinct angle to what would be a normal, erect, standing posture.

If your lower body is too stiff and inflexible, you will tend to sway during the golf swing. If your upper body is too erect, your shoulders will tend to turn on too horizontal a plane during the swing for your particular stature, instead of simultaneously turning and tilting—a

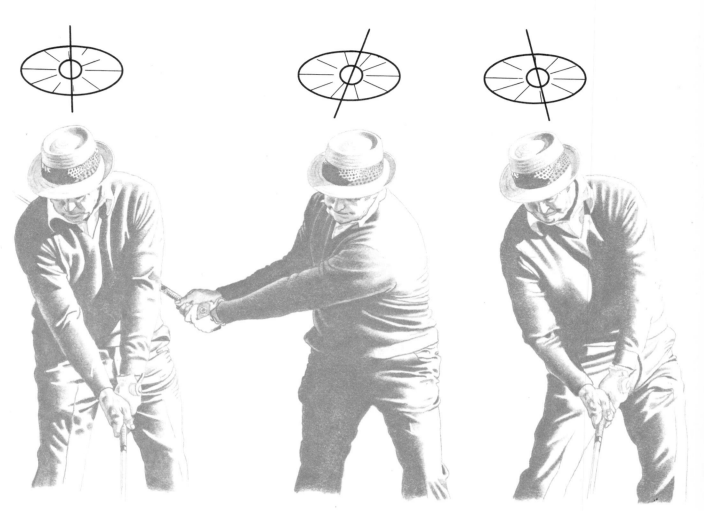

BODY KEY 2 HEAD IS SWING HUB

Your head should never be held so firmly positioned that you can feel strain in your neck muscles. Rather, it should swivel freely during the swing around a natural fixed point. The Happy Hacker demonstrates the two most common head faults—swaying away from the ball on the backswing, and toward the target on the downswing. Both moves wreck the swing arc.

combination action that is present in all turns and that naturally varies somewhat with height and build.

Standing up to the ball "in halves" is the key to avoiding such problems, and to establishing a truly natural, balanced, and "ready" golf posture without having to go through a dozen geometrical contortions.

BODY KEY 2: YOUR HEAD IS YOUR SWING HUB

I never thought much about my head position when I was learning to play golf. I saw it as serving like the hub of a wheel and realized that it had to function thus by remaining at the center of my swing action. I also noticed that a steady head position became more important the closer I got to the flag, until, with a short putt, I had the feeling that my head had to be as immovable as the Rock of Gibraltar or the stroke would surely be lost.

You can overdo "head still," however, especially if by thinking of it overconsciously you tend to freeze your neck muscles and thereby prevent the small but vital swiveling action of the chin on the backswing that I and many other top pros use—Jack Nicklaus's chin swivel is a very pronounced example—to enable us to make a free, full body turn. What we do is set our heads behind the ball, then, just before or as we start to swing, we swivel the chin a little more to the right and then keep it there through impact. That simple device gets you out of your own way and gives your shoulders maximum room to coil while still allowing you to swing around a fixed axis (which actually becomes the back of the neck).

This preliminary action might be especially important to short and/or heavy-set golfers, who are limited in the degree of turn they can make with their bodies, and so must maximize their opportunity to turn.

Instead of *swiveling* the head, many golfers have a tendency to let it *sway* away from the target during the backswing. I think that fault, which upsets the swing arc and destroys balance, originates in an unconscious desire to let the head move back with the hands during the takeaway, since head and hands are aligned at address. If you think of the back of your neck staying with the *ball* while your hands move back with the club head, you'll be in good shape.

Likewise on the downswing, the head must stay in its original position in relation to the ball if the swing arc and plane are not to be changed. The head must stay back and down with the shot until the ball is well on its way.

BODY KEY 3: YOUR ARMS ESTABLISH THE ARC

Your arms play a major part in swinging the club away from the ball in a wide, smooth arc—*and in making the same arc each time you swing.*

If you think of bringing the firm left arm up to a point midway between your head and right shoulder at the completion of the backswing, and then the straightening right arm up midway between your head and left shoulder on the follow-through, you cannot fail to develop a good, full swing arc.

Your left arm must remain firm and extended throughout the swing, from takeaway until after impact, if your arc is to remain consistent, so it makes sense to have it that way at address. Always check to see that the left arm makes a nice, straight extension with the club itself, without going to the point of making it ramrod rigid. If it is rigid at address, it will tend to break down later in the swing.

Think of your left arm as a compass drawing the outline of a circle on a piece of drafting paper. The arm moves up and around and then down and around in a straight, sweeping motion. Don't do anything unnatural to break the smooth arc it describes. Remember, the hands operate at the end of your arm. If the elbow bends, you wind up with two hinges in your swing, not just one.

Make sure you feel the upper part of the left arm—from the elbow to the shoulder—pressed lightly against your side as you begin the backswing. If it's hanging away from your body, you're reaching too far for the ball, or the elbow is bent.

The left arm wants to buckle when it's under the most pressure. That's at the top of the backswing, at the start of the downswing, and at impact. When that happens, your swing arc changes, necessitating some lightning-fast hand work to get the club head on the ball. Not many golfers can handle such compensations, which is another reason for establishing a firm-but-not-rigid left arm at address and consciously keeping it that way throughout the swing.

Some golfers find that they cannot keep the left arm perfectly straight at the top of the swing unless they actually make it rigid, which in turn practically guarantees that the arm will bend on the downswing. In such a case, it is much better to let the arm give a little at the top, and to rely on centrifugal force's outward pull to straighten it coming down. Keeping the left arm straight throughout the hitting area is, however, vital to solid shot making.

When you're making solid contact with the ball, you will feel the shot right up your left forearm at impact. If you're missing that sensation altogether, chances are your left arm is breaking down somewhere —usually on the way down.

The right arm never feels busy in a good golf swing. So, at address, relax it. Keep it comfortably flexed, with the elbow close to your side but not consciously pressed in there.

During the backswing, the right arm naturally moves away from the side somewhat, and if you try to keep the elbow stuck to your ribs you're never going to be able to take the club back as fully as you need to achieve the distance you'd like. But don't go to the other extreme of

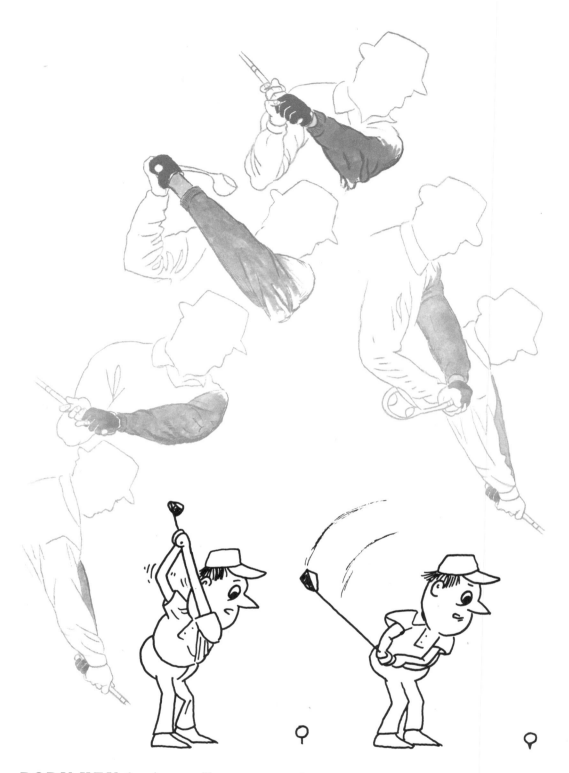

BODY KEY 3 ARMS ESTABLISH ARC

The left arm serves as a kind of compass arm in the good golf swing, enabling the club head to describe the swing arc that is most natural for the individual golfer. Too straight or too bent a left arm—see Happy—creates an unnatural, and thus an inconsistent, arc.

lifting the elbow miles away from your side, because that will tend to give too much influence to the right hand at the start of the downswing, and your chances of hitting a good shot will be cut in half.

One way to get the feeling of keeping the right elbow in comfortably close is to stick a club-head cover under your arm and practice swinging that way for a while. Another way is to have the feeling of letting the right elbow *sweep* along your side.

A good position at the top of the backswing sets the right arm directly *under* the club—exactly as a busboy holds his arm while carrying a tray of dishes—with the elbow pointing directly at the ground. Coming down, the right elbow must move back in close to the rib cage, and to consciously feel it doing so is a good way to prevent "hitting from the top," or "hitting too early," with the hands and wrists. Concentrating on bringing the right elbow back into your side at the start of the downswing will also help you to keep your right hand from grabbing control of the club too soon—something that you're always going to have to fight if you've been a congenital slicer or puller of the ball.

BODY KEY 4: YOUR HIPS AND SHOULDERS COIL IN TANDEM

I am treating hips and shoulders under one body key to emphasize a point: *Hips and shoulders must work in tandem to ensure a full and fluid body turn with no snags or hitches.*

The old instructional concept of turning your body in a barrel, away from the target on the backswing and toward the target on the downswing, is a good mental picture for developing proper hip-and-shoulder action, because it encourages you to rotate and coil, rather than sway or lift, in getting the club back and down. I also like the image because a "barrel" is big enough to keep hips and shoulders together, where they belong.

115

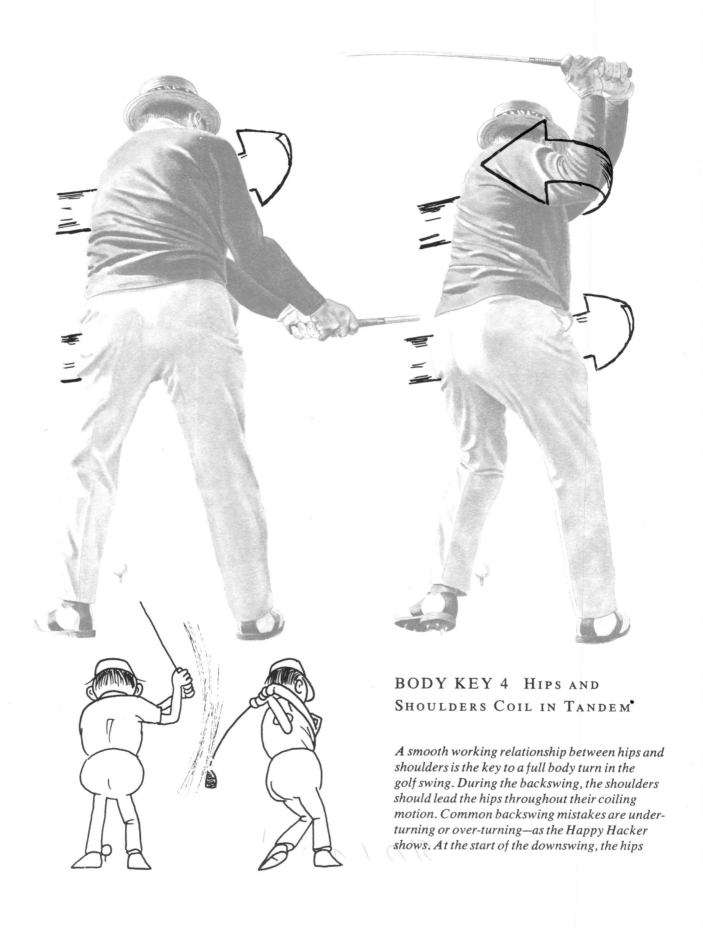

BODY KEY 4 HIPS AND SHOULDERS COIL IN TANDEM

A smooth working relationship between hips and shoulders is the key to a full body turn in the golf swing. During the backswing, the shoulders should lead the hips throughout their coiling motion. Common backswing mistakes are under-turning or over-turning—as the Happy Hacker shows. At the start of the downswing, the hips

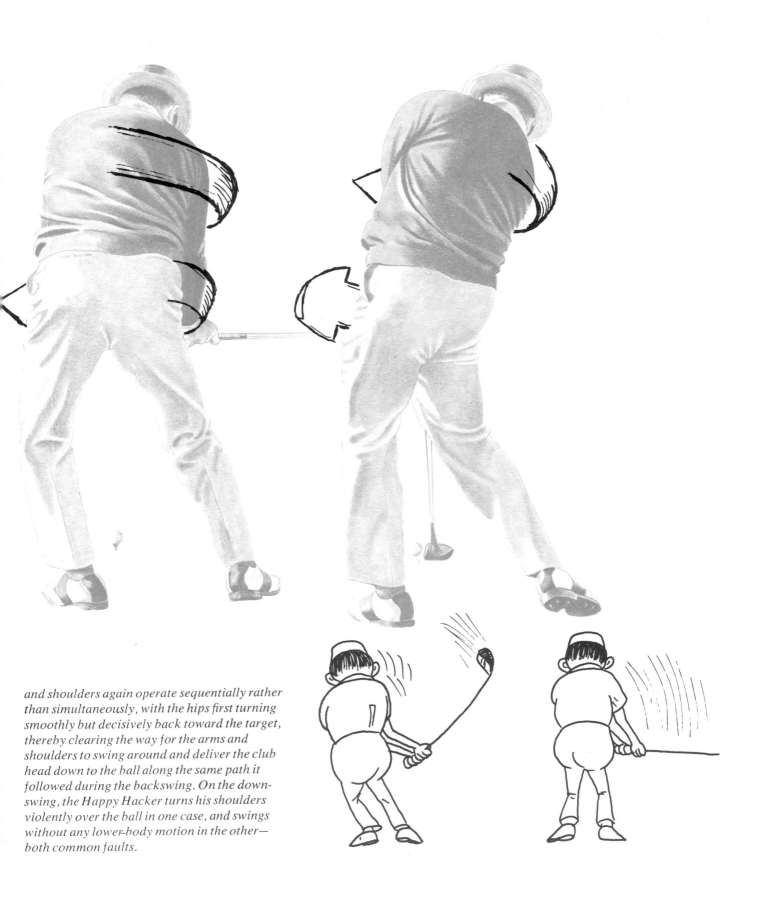

and shoulders again operate sequentially rather than simultaneously, with the hips first turning smoothly but decisively back toward the target, thereby clearing the way for the arms and shoulders to swing around and deliver the club head down to the ball along the same path it followed during the backswing. On the down-swing, the Happy Hacker turns his shoulders violently over the ball in one case, and swings without any lower-body motion in the other—both common faults.

The shoulder turn should *never* be separated from the hip turn during the swing. Each builds naturally on the other. For example, if you turn your hips but don't turn your shoulders enough, you shorten your swing arc considerably. Conversely, if you're supple enough to be able to turn your hips but not your shoulders, you create a lot of unnecessary tension in your body and thereby risk all kinds of downswing faults.

Shuttling your backside to the rear in standing up to the ball, as described earlier when we were talking about posture, helps set your hips in a position at address from which they can turn freely but firmly.

The shoulders at address must be considered at greater length. Many golfers feel awkward in their shoulders from the very first time they put a golf club behind a ball, because their instincts tell them to set their shoulders level to the ground—in other words, horizontal—yet the act of gripping the club with the right hand lower on the handle than the left automatically causes the shoulder line to slant slightly away from the target. You must allow nature to take its course in this element of the setup. Trying to level the shoulders at address can cause all kinds of faults, including pushing the hands too far forward and hooding the club face. Worse, it gets a golfer into the habit of turning his shoulders *around* (on a horizontal plane) rather than *under and around* (on a plane between horizontal and vertical) during both the backswing and downswing. So, before anything else, make sure that your shoulders tilt naturally away from the target at address, in sympathy with the position of your right hand sitting lower on the club than your left.

After you make your forward press, you should feel that your hips and shoulders are starting away from the ball *together,* as the takeaway begins. Don't leave either one at the starting gate, as often happens in a careless or lazy beginning to the swing. At the same time, beware of twisting your hips and shoulders sharply away from the target as an initiating backswing action. Rather, let both turn naturally in synchronization with and in response to your hand and arm motion as the club is swung back and up.

During the backswing, the shoulders, possessing the broader axis, should begin to feel more active than the hips in their turning or coiling motion. A good way to get the shoulders to turn as fully as they should is to concentrate on bringing the left shoulder around from its address position until it is pointing at the ball.

Recognize that your shoulders must tilt as they turn, and that they will tilt more and more in relation to their turning action as the club shafts shorten and you necessarily stand closer to the ball. This tilt occurs naturally with all clubs when you reach for a high hand position —for the power slot—at the top of your backswing. If you don't have any tilt in your shoulder turn, it means that you are swinging on a very flat plane to a low hand position, giving yourself a lot less leverage to work with. From the resulting top-of-the-backswing position, you're also going to have a hard time delivering the club head squarely into the ball.

When the shoulders are turned and tilted properly, your left shoulder will be beneath your chin at the top of your swing and your back will be fully toward the target.

It's important to check your turn regularly to make sure that it is not easing up on you, or that you're not easing up on it. There seems to be a natural tendency among most golfers for the hips and shoulders to become less active and for the arms and hands to do more and more of the work. When that happens, all the power of the body goes out of the swing and pretty soon all you're doing is flicking at the ball with just your fingers and wrists.

At the start of the downswing, the hips and shoulders operate more *in sequence* than simultaneously, with the hips first turning decisively back toward the target, thereby clearing the way for your arms and shoulders to swing around and deliver the club down to the ball along the same path it followed during the backswing.

That initial hip movement on the downswing may give you the feeling of "sitting down" slightly, especially if you jam your left heel into the turf, as I recommend, as a way of getting the weight shifting smartly back toward the target. This "sitting down" sensation is valuable because it indicates that you're not spinning out of your natural pivot with too much hip movement as the downswing gets under way. Due to the force involved in the downswing, the hips are inclined to go a little bit more forward of the position they occupied at address, but that is not something for conscious thought, because if the rest of your moves are sound it will happen automatically.

The shoulder action during the downswing is purely reflexive. If your shoulders swing around on the same plane they turned and tilted on during the backswing, your right shoulder will be correctly tucked under your chin at the moment of impact.

Every golfer can turn his hips and shoulders only to the limits imposed by his individual build and suppleness, but within those limits he can usually maximize that turn by developing certain points of emphasis.

If you're tall, you'll simply have more body to turn with from the waist up than the short person, and you should take advantage of that by stressing the coiling of your shoulders and building good leverage in the upright swing plane that will be natural to you. Your shoulders will turn "under" more than normal in the backswing if you are making good use of your frame.

If you're on the short side, you must emphasize turning the hips, along with striving for a high hand position, in order to get a good extension away from the ball and so get more leverage into your swing. You should also allow your left heel to raise off the ground on the backswing (as will be described in more detail in Body Key 6). Your shoulders will turn "around" more than a taller golfer's do—but do not let them turn any more flatly than you must.

If you're unusually thin, you should guard against turning *too* much, with the resultant danger that you do not shift your weight sharply back toward the target in starting down. If you're unusually chubby, you will not be able to turn fully in either direction, so your main concern should be to preserve your balance by extending only within your limits. A fat golfer usually can play much more effectively by keeping his weight on the left side throughout the swing, shortening his backswing, and keeping his right arm tucked well into his side.

Before every round or practice session, I "oil" my turn by placing a club across my back, looping my arms around it, and turning my hips and shoulders back and forth a dozen times in a replica of the action I want during the swing. Besides reminding me of the feeling of a full windup, this exercise also loosens up my arm, shoulder, and back muscles so that I'm less likely to strain anything once I actually start to hit balls. It's a good oiling device for golfers of any build.

BODY KEY 5: FLEXED KNEES KEEP THE SWING FLUID

Use your knees to keep your lower body in gear throughout the swing.

Lightly flex and relax your knees at address and you'll be off to a good start. During a round or practice session, you might also lubricate those joints from time to time with a few shallow knee bends.

Practice the swing in slow motion with your hands in your pockets and watch what your knees do. As your weight rolls to the inside of your right foot, your left knee will want to bend in, toward the ball. Then, on the downswing, as the weight rolls back to your left foot, your *right* knee will naturally seek to bend in toward the ball. Encourage that key thrusting motion coming down because, given good timing, it can add many yards to your shots.

The worst thing you can do with your knees is stiffen them at any point during the swing. Whenever there is movement, the knees must be flexed—"easy" in their sockets. A locked right knee on the backswing freezes up the whole right side and almost forces you to throw your shoulders and the club forward from the top. It's by far the most common knee fault, even among good golfers, and it's a deadly fault, because it prevents the player from using his legs and hips to shift to his left side for a proper hit.

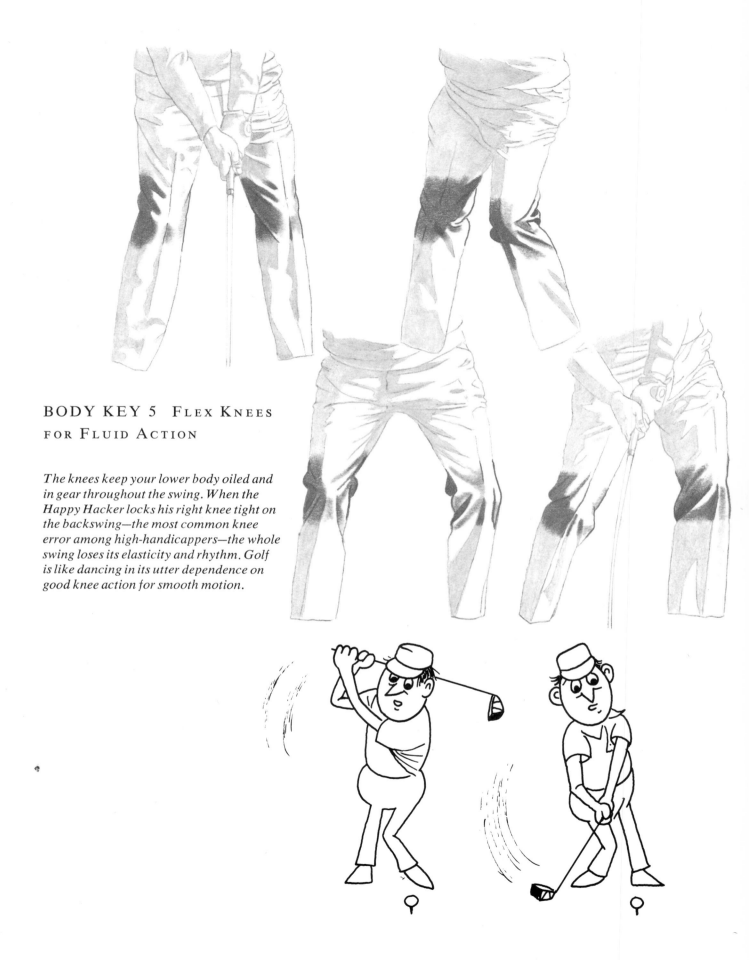

BODY KEY 5 FLEX KNEES FOR FLUID ACTION

The knees keep your lower body oiled and in gear throughout the swing. When the Happy Hacker locks his right knee tight on the backswing—the most common knee error among high-handicappers—the whole swing loses its elasticity and rhythm. Golf is like dancing in its utter dependence on good knee action for smooth motion.

Try a walk across the room, or a waltz, with your knees locked in their sockets and see how hard it is to move around freely. Same problem develops in your golf swing unless you keep your knee joints nice and flexible. When you have good knee action, hitting a golf ball is as smooth as riding over a bump in the road in a car with super shock absorbers.

BODY KEY 6: YOUR FEET GOVERN THE PIVOT

It is true that I've practiced barefooted at times to correct problems with my balance and my pivot—which shows how much I value good footwork in the swing. After all, your feet are your only contact with the ground. They support your body weight and make or break your balance when that weight is shifted during the swing. To me, the feet are so important that I check them before anything else whenever I seem to be losing touch with my swing.

Your feet should give you the feeling of being solidly anchored, both at address and during the swing, with the pressure of your weight felt between the balls and heels of your feet. That placement of weight is key because (1) it prevents you from falling forward into the swing, and (2) it allows you to draw on your big hitting muscles, which are located more on the back side of your physique than toward the front. It's a setup that allows you to move from side to side with the same kind of balance you need for Indian wrestling.

The pressure of your body weight should also be felt more on the *insides* of your golf shoes than on the outsides. Thinking of "weighing in" at address helps to center the body in this manner, and is the key to staying totally in balance throughout the swing. "Weighing in" also reduces your chances of swaying laterally off the ball on either the backswing or the downswing, both of which are common mistakes. Pinching your knees in toward each other a little is the simple way to bring the

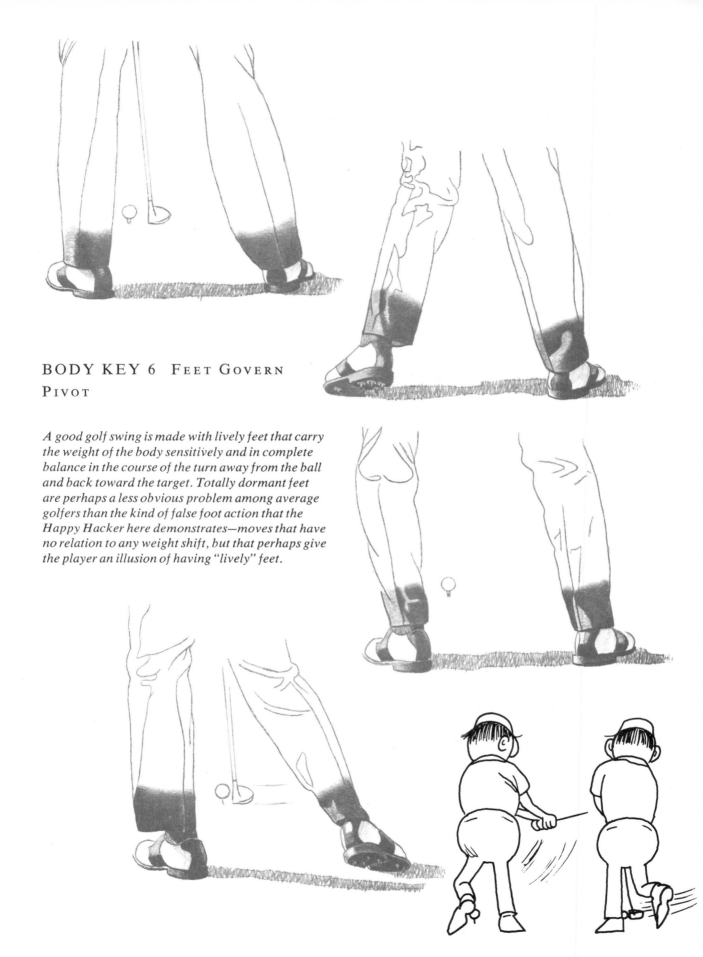

BODY KEY 6 FEET GOVERN PIVOT

A good golf swing is made with lively feet that carry the weight of the body sensitively and in complete balance in the course of the turn away from the ball and back toward the target. Totally dormant feet are perhaps a less obvious problem among average golfers than the kind of false foot action that the Happy Hacker here demonstrates—moves that have no relation to any weight shift, but that perhaps give the player an illusion of having "lively" feet.

bulk of your weight onto the insides of your feet.

Once you know how to control weight distribution through foot action, winding and unwinding the body fully and powerfully becomes easy. As an exercise, practice rolling your weight from one foot to the other to give yourself the feeling of the shifts in weight that take place during the swing.

Of course, you can't roll your feet properly if they are uncomfortably angled in your stance, nor can you roll them if there's no liveliness in them. Many pivot problems can be traced to leaden or dormant feet. Sometimes golfers try so hard to build a solid stance that they almost glue their feet into the ground and thereby cut them out of the swing entirely. Anchor your feet, not to freeze your body action but to give yourself a lively and resilient base for springy, fluid movement. Particularly, don't be afraid of your left heel leaving the ground as your backswing progresses. There's no way to make a full pivot of the shoulders and hips and keep that left heel on the ground unless you are very tall or miraculously supple.

On the backswing, allow your weight to shift to the *inside* of the rear foot in your stance in response to your shoulder and hip turn, and no farther. That way your hips and shoulders can neither sway nor overswing, but will be forced to coil and pivot your body to get the club back—the only way to build distance-producing leverage. At this point, your left foot will merely be a prop for your weight.

As the downswing begins with the pulling downward of the club handle by the last two fingers of the left hand, jam that upraised left heel back into the ground *very hard,* toward the target. That's the best single move I know to get your legs and hips to move your weight back to your left side, where it must be if you are to strike the ball accurately and powerfully.

I feel like my right foot really digs in during the downswing, too, but without the heel coming off the ground until after impact. If that happens, I will have spun my body too quickly and will hit both short and wild.

1 2 : Tips for Better Timing

NOT long ago I was watching a fellow trying to slam the cover off the ball on the practice tee.

"Treat that ball a little more gently!" I said. I grabbed his club and demonstrated. "Swing to waltz time—la-la-la . . . la-la-*boom!*"

"I know something about waltz time," the pupil declared. "Believe it or not, I'm a professional dancer!"

"You are? Well, stop swinging to a fast foxtrot like you've been doing, and swing to waltz time instead!"

That tip changed his golf swing from terrible to pretty fair in five seconds.

The incident shows what a difference good timing, or rhythm, can make in golf. It also points up the fact that most golfers are inclined to swing too *fast* rather than too slow—to a quick step or a rock 'n' roll cadence, for instance, rather than to a waltz beat. In fact, I don't think I could name a dozen golfers I ever saw swinging too slowly for their own good.

Good timing may be a cinch to understand if you're a professional dancer, such as my pupil, whose whole life is spent keeping his body in motion in a rhythmic manner. But many weekend golfers overlook or misunderstand various aspects of good timing—primarily, I believe, because it is one of the conditions for success in golf that lies outside the strict province of mechanical technique. Yet, without it, the mechanical actions fall apart. It is what brings together the action positions of the hands with the key movements of the body during the swing. More often than not, trying to get good timing in my swing is the only thing that's on my mind when I step up to the ball.

Good timing makes it possible for the club head to meet the ball at the bottom of the swing arc, with the club head moving at top speed and the bulk of the golfer's weight packed behind the shot. You hear a well-timed shot before its results show up down the fairway. When the club head slaps into the back of the ball, there is a very sharp, re-sounding crack. If, instead, the club head is moved through the impact area too slowly, there is a dull, thudlike, muted sound. And a really mis-hit wood shot sometimes sounds as bad as a broken-bat single in baseball.

There's not much point in concentrating very heavily on building good timing until you have developed at least some mastery of the foundations, and are well on your way to grooving your swing through hand and body keys. And while in the course of that work you will instinctively develop a sense of what good timing is, you will, even so, frequently find yourself apparently doing everything right in your swing, yet spraying shots wildly. That's when you should step back and attack the problem from the fresh perspective of timing.

To help you in that, here are my basic keys for creating a well-paced swing. In explaining them, I'll occasionally have to repeat things mentioned earlier in this section. But I will be doing so only to point out and explain as clearly as possible what I consider to be the main elements in good timing. So bear with me and focus on the main objective, which is building good timing in your own game.

swinging in a slower, easier rhythm.

Warning: When you cut your physical exertion down to 85 percent, don't make the mistake of cutting your swing back, too, or your body will stop working correctly with the swing you have grooved. I've seen touring pros throw off their timing in this manner, particularly when playing a course with unusually narrow fairways. The tight landing areas make the pros unconsciously shorten up on their swings to keep the ball in play. Then, when they get to a more open course down the road, they start spraying their drives wildly without knowing why. The reason is that their turn, cut back to three-quarters of normal, no longer suits their tempo. Their arm swing is too fast for their reduced pivot, and their shots fly all over the park.

3. START BACK SLOW AND PAUSE AT THE TOP

It's the long shots that bring out the killer instinct in many a golfer, and totally disrupt tempo—another commonly used word for good timing. Yet it's the full shots with the long clubs that require more time to execute, and therefore better timing to execute well. The longer the club, the slower the backswing has to be, and the more deliberately the downswing must begin. There's a kind of "double delay" built into the well-timed swing. Why? I would explain it as follows.

The driver, for instance, being the longest club in the bag, has the longest path to travel, as it extends away and up from the ball. Unless you give yourself time to wind the club up into its fullest arc, you will not be able to obtain the distance that is built into the club.

A lot of golfers think that the faster they take the club back, the faster it will fly through the ball. The opposite is true. Too quick a backswing tends to cut your club head speed coming down, in that your hand and body actions never have time to synchronize.

It might help your timing if you consider these two analogies.

1. In making a long throw from the outfield, a baseball player swings his arm back in a deliberate, gathering-of-forces manner that is slow, relative to the speed at which he moves the arm forward. At the last moment in his throw forward, his wrist uncocks and flings the ball off his fingertips at top speed.

2. In driving a nail, the carpenter brings his hammer up slowly, and throws it down upon the head of the nail fast.

In both these actions the first phase of the "swing" requires a longer time period than the second phase. The same holds for swinging a golf club effectively.

The start of the backswing is especially critical, because that's when the basic rhythm or pace of the swing is established. Taking the club back with the conscious feeling of pushing it deliberately along the takeaway track with the left hand may help you build a slower, smoother action.

If the swing *up* is accomplished with a proper gathering of the forces in the body, then the swing *down* must put those forces to use in some orderly way. Pausing momentarily at the top sets up this orderly use. It's kind of like leaving the club up there on the shelf for a fraction of a second. My feeling of reaching to a high hand position at the top of the swing helps to create the pause. So does the thought, "Wait till you're ready!" Anything's good that gives you enough time for the body forces to begin to uncoil and to get a head start over the club head. The club head will move down mighty fast, anyway, because of centrifugal force. Given a head start, the body forces are able to unload into the ball at the same time as the club head.

Remember, yardage in a golf shot is produced not by speed of execution (how fast you swing) but by club head speed at time of impact —which is a function of *how* you swing. And maximum club head speed at impact is created as the result of a kind of double delay: first when you extend the club back fully and deliberately, and then when you let your wrists whip the club into the ball at the last possible moment.

4. SWING DOWN ON THE LINE YOU SWING UP ON

Try to swing your club down along the same path on which you swung it back.

That suggestion has worked wonders for golfers with timing problems, especially more advanced players whose backswings are basically good already. It's the key I use most frequently when my timing goes off.

If you can swing the club back down to the ball on the same path that it followed as you swung it up to the top, you succeed in *simplifying* your golf swing by immediately reducing or eliminating any loops and flourishes that may have crept into your game and made your timing erratic. Instead of jerking the club inside, or throwing it outside, you keep the club on line in the groove that is right for you.

For the sake of any mechanical purists who may be reading this book, I suppose I should mention here that no good golfer does actually *exactly* reproduce his backswing path with his downswing path. Because of the shifting of weight targetward that comes from lower body action, and the increased cocking of the wrists resulting from the initiating moves of the downswing, the club head actually travels down to the ball more steeply and usually a little more from the "inside" than it traveled back. But this is beside the point. What I'm suggesting is a *mental picture* of the paths being identical, because it is a thought that almost always improves a player's timing.

133

5. HOW TO SENSE WELL-TIMED HAND ACTION

Your timing will improve the moment you understand that you must let power happen in your swing, rather than try to force it to happen.

Good timing is developed out of the *indirect*, not direct, sensation of shaft flex and club-head momentum.

To see exactly what I mean, take a long flexible stick and impale an apple on it. Experiment with whipping the stick through the air so that the stick bends and then snaps forward, and the apple comes loose from the stick and flies toward some target. With a little practice you'll be able to gauge the kind of hand action you need to make the apple hit a target. But the feeling you'll recognize and then cultivate is not one of "hand throwing apple," but of "hand whipping stick so that apple will come loose." The "apple coming loose" part is an *indirect* sensation—almost more an observation than a feeling.

Same in golf. You whip the club around so that the shaft bends and then swings straight, and as a result the club head flies forward with a spurt of speed at just the right moment. You don't feel the club head jumping at the ball in the sense that you would if your hands were directly participating in the action, as they were in swinging the club up to that point. Something happens that is literally "out of your hands," that being the burst of club-head speed, indirectly felt, that produces extra distance on your shots.

6. KEEP YOUR LEGS LIVELY

Good timing is a product of the entire swing motion and not just one or two parts of the hand or body actions. But many golfers find that focusing on one movement of the body, or one action of the hands, helps to build overall rhythm.

I've already mentioned, for example, the "double delay" actions as useful to building rhythm. Some of the hand and body keys can do the same thing for some golfers. For instance, I think my timing is helped at the start of the downswing by the key action position of pulling down on the club with the last two fingers of my left hand. I've said that helps keep my right hand from becoming too active too soon. In a way, the last two fingers of my left hand are a focal point for my sense of rhythm—a kind of bandleader's baton—holding up the drums while the violin finishes.

The danger in settling on one key hand or body action for timing is that occasionally the rest of the swing actions may go dead—get out of sync with the consciously performed key action. Your "baton," in directing one section of the band, may forget about the other sections, and the piece won't get played right. That's why I always stress over-all rhythm in my thoughts—everything moving together—even when I'm focusing on one part of the dance.

The lower body, especially, must remain alert and lively throughout the swing for good timing to occur. If the legs or feet go to sleep, the pivot changes, which changes the path of the club head by changing the path of the hands and arms both going back and coming down.

Years ago Toney Penna was having trouble with his tempo, and he asked me for help. I could see that his feet were acting kind of dead in the swing, so I suggested he think of hitting the ball with the feet during his swing. The idea of swinging that way worked like a dream

—it restored a lively, rolling action to his feet and put the rhythm back into both his windup and unwind.

I've heard golfers—starting with Walter Hagen back in the 1930s all the way to Jack Nicklaus here in the 1970s—complain about their legs feeling dead on certain days, and not being able to play worth a damn as a result. That's why I recommend a lively walking style and occasional knee bends during a round—in fact, anything to keep your feet and legs alert and limber.

Part IV
COMPETING

13: Three Swings in One— How to Simplify as You Go

IN this section I want to shift my emphasis from the job of swinging the golf club correctly to that of scoring halfway decently on the golf course.

A good golf swing is small satisfaction if you can't break 100 with it (and half of all golfers can't break 100, as we pointed out at the start of this book), or if you're stuck in the 90s when you have the potential to shoot in the 80s, or stuck in the 80s when you could shoot 79 or better.

Don't get me wrong—the swing comes first. But after you've grooved a golf swing, you still have to master the on-course tactics and techniques that will get you around eighteen holes in the fewest possible number of strokes.

Scoring low in golf boils down to competing effectively against your course, your opponents, and yourself. Those are the areas we'll concentrate on in this section. In particular, we'll try to get you to manage your long game better, sharpen your approach shots, learn to putt the greens more "conservatively," and, finally, isolate the mental and emotional traits you need to win at golf.

Before getting into specifics, though, let me explain generally how that grooved swing of yours must be slightly *tailored* to meet the conditions of actual play. In point of fact, golf demands three distinct sizes of swing from tee to green—a full swing, a medium swing, and a short swing—with each one being just that little bit more compact and precise the closer you get to the target.

A good analogy to this "three swings in one" concept might be the fellow with three suits of clothes—one for business, one for social gatherings, and a third for formal affairs. Each suit fits fine and is comfortable, and beneath all three suits is the same frame. But each suit serves a particular function, and looks and feels different when worn.

The basic framework of the golf swing never changes from tee to green, but it is altered in *feeling* by slight differences in swing arc and weight positioning. Once you understand these differences, and learn to apply them, your overall game will become both simpler and sharper.

Let me now describe the full swing, medium swing, and short swing, point out the special shot conditions that dictate the three variations, and try to convey the feelings and sensations unique to each.

THE FULL SWING

By the full swing I mean primarily the swing you make with the driver from the tee. It's the biggest swing, with the longest and least-lofted club, and with maximum yardage as its number-one goal.

Throw Your Weight Behind the Shot. There's a saying, "Tee off with pounds, putt with ounces." Applying your body weight for all it's worth is one of the most beneficial sensations you can develop in your full swing. The whole body is involved in turning, stretching, and, finally unleashing. If it's not, chances are you're never going to develop the leverage necessary to achieve your full potential distance.

Set up for the tee shot so that the bulk of your weight is *behind* the ball, with the ball positioned off your left heel in the stance. That setup gives you extra thrust as you turn into the shot. Actually, the trick is to be sure your head is always positioned *behind* the ball, which enables you to turn entirely behind the ball so that at the moment of impact your entire weight is behind the club.

Stay on Your Feet. The big arc and pronounced weight shift of the full swing calls for extra good balance. That requires setting up to the ball with careful attention to weight distribution. Stress the feeling of "sitting down" in the stance at address—sticking out your posterior and keeping your knees good and flexed so that your weight is centered more toward your heels than your toes.

Also, pinch in those knees a bit—make yourself feel a little knock-kneed—in order to get the weight to ride more on the insides of your feet than one the outsides. That will discourage swaying off the ball.

Sweep Through. The ball is teed up for driving, which encourages you to swing with a more sweeping than pinching action. The idea is for the club head to meet the ball at or just fractionally past the bottom of the swing arc, so that it is hit *directly forward*. If you position the ball too far back in your stance, you'll tend to hit down on the ball and thereby greatly reduce both its carry and roll. Remember, the relatively straight-faced driver is designed to hit the ball much more *forward* than up, which it can only do when the ball is positioned forward and hit with a sweeping rather than a chopping action.

Start Slow for Good Timing. The more distance you're going for on a shot, the longer it takes to wind up the club to produce the leverage you need to create maximum club-head speed. On the driver swing, the length of the shaft calls for a little extra time on the way back, and the big weight shift demands more time on the way down. Remember that your entire tempo will be established by the manner in which the club head travels the first couple of feet back from the ball. The most consciously deliberate takeaway you can produce is the one that will work best, especially with the driver.

THE MEDIUM SWING

The medium swing is the swing made off grass—without benefit of a teed ball—with the fairway woods, long irons, and medium irons.

Trust the Club. Lack of faith in their equipment is a very common cause of high scores among amateur golfers. It is nowhere more evident than in the problems these players have in using the longer-shafted clubs from the fairway. A ball lying in grass, rather than sitting up on a wooden peg, just does not seem accessible to them, and the comparatively small amount of loft built into the faces of the long-shafted clubs just doesn't seem sufficient to make the ball rise.

Thus players approach the long fairway shots with the conscious or subconscious idea that the club is going to require a lot of extra help and manipulation from them if the ball is to rise into the air and fly any distance. One result is overuse of the hands in trying to manipulate the ball into the air. Another is swinging too fast. Understand that there is, indeed, a fractional increase in the speed of the swing, due to the slight decrease in the length of the club shaft as the clubs shorten, but that this variable is not something you must try to create deliberately. In fact, the same deliberate tempo you use on the tee shot is the best tempo to try to seek in swinging your fairway woods and long irons.

142

Only experience—and work on the practice tee—will convey to most golfers the total effectiveness of *all* their clubs in getting the ball airborne.

Strike Down to Hit Up. If the full swing is a sweeping action, the fairway swing is more of a pinching action, in which, ideally, the club head strikes the ball just before the club reaches the bottom of its arc.

Catching the ball as it is still traveling slightly downward, the club head causes the ball to roll up its face, imparting all the backspin that is necessary to get it airborne. Properly applied, the club head does the job, not the golfer.

Take a Divot in Front of the Ball. A divot is a piece of turf skinned loose by the leading edge of the club head *after* it has hit the ball. Golfers who exaggerate the downward blow of the fairway swing— usually by having the ball too far forward in the stance—often take divots before their club has made contact with the ball. The divot mark starts behind where the ball lay, and is a clear indicator of wasted power. Taking a divot in *front* of the ball is the result of meeting the ball at the correct point in the swing arc. Thus, a shallow divot mark in front of where the ball lay actually represents the true bottom of the fairway swing arc.

When your divots appear behind the ball rather than in front of it, the fault lies either in your stance or your downswing. The ball may be positioned too far forward. Or you may be lunging at the ball from the top, or scooping at it with your hands, because you are overanxious about getting the shot airborne.

Some golfers are afraid to take divots because they think doing so requires a lot of extra force. Some even worry vaguely about hurting themselves. In actual fact, the sharp bottom edge of any iron club flying at the speed of the average golf swing becomes more than forceful enough to cut effortlessly through any turf.

THE SHORT SWING

The short swing is made with the accuracy clubs—for most golfers, the six iron on down. Now you're shooting for the flag—for the section of the green where the cup is located, unless there's an intervening hazard that you would rather not flirt with.

Short and Solid. The feeling of the short swing is simpler, more compressed, and naturally a little faster (although always smooth). As the distance the ball must travel is reduced, the length of the club shaft is lessened and the backswing is instinctively shortened proportionately. At the top of the backswing with the short irons, because the golfer necessarily stands closer to the ball, the club is also naturally in a more upright plane than with the longer clubs.

Your Weight Stays on the Left. Since the length of the club does not dictate a long, flowing arc, there is no need for the big body turn and weight shift that was the carrier for the long arc on the full swing and the fairway swing. In fact, on most shots the short swing is so compressed, comparatively, that a substantial weight shift can wreck the action. By keeping your weight on your left side throughout the swing, you minimize the weight shift and simplify the swing without robbing it of power and accuracy.

So the main characteristic of the short swing, to me, is a feeling that the bulk of the weight is on the left side at address, with the right leg serving primarily simply as a "prop" in the stance. Here you can generate most of the limited power you need through arm-and-hand speed, and it makes sense to limit lower body action—for example, the left heel need never leave the ground, as it must for most players in order to pivot properly during the full swing.

When you establish the bulk of your weight on your left side at address, you make sure that your weight will be where you want it when you bring the club head crisply and solidly down and through the ball.

Keep Your Upper Body Firm. Since the arms and hands are generating most of the force in the short swing, it is especially important to use them firmly and positively. In other words, don't let the relative inactivity of the lower body creep into the upper body. On short shots, it is particularly important to remain conscious of keeping your left arm straight and your right elbow tucked well into your side. Also, try to avoid any sensation of slackness in your grip and your wrists.

Play the Shot "Close to Your Vest." On all normal short shots the ball is played near to the center of the stance. Avoid playing the ball too far forward, as many hackers do, or you will hit behind the ball. Don't forget that, as on the long irons, the ball must always be struck before the club head contacts the ground.

Many golfers tend to set up to the short shots with the ball too far away from the body. The closer you get to the green, the more control over the shot you need, and the closer you can stand to the ball and still remain comfortable, the more control you will have over the swing.

Firmness in the upper body includes a good, steady head position. Again, since the short swing is mainly an upper-body swing, the head position becomes crucial. Concentrate on keeping your head over the ball more than you might normally do on other shots.

Trust the Club. Golfers tend to want to help short shots along by scooping at the ball. Firm hand action and faith in the club face loft will keep you from missing the little shots to the green.

14: How to Manage Your Long Shots

THE three major factors in effectively managing your long game are targeting off the tee correctly, keeping up your concentration for the second shot, and learning to cope with unusual lies.

TARGETING OFF THE TEE

Every shot has its own value, relative to the level of play of the individual golfer. For the pros there's no question but that putting is the single most important stroke in golf, especially these days. But for many golfers putting should not be regarded as the most important stroke. Rather, driving should be placed first.

I emphasize driving, not because I've always had a reputation as a good driver, but because I've seen so many amateurs knock their tee shots in the direction of all fifty states on any given Saturday morning, and thereby make a good score impossible.

The value of the driver cannot be overestimated in the play of the average golfer, simply because it has such a crucial effect on the play of the rest of each hole. The tee shot starts you off right, or it starts you off wrong. By getting started on every long hole with a drive that leaves you in a position from which you can play directly onto or toward the green, you build the confidence you need to apply the technique required for the second shot.

In some ways the drive should be the easiest shot in golf. The ball is teed up to your specification every time, the stance is always level, and the swing itself is "automated." With fewer variables, there should be fewer errors. Yet driving is a problem for most ordinary golfers, and if you're one of them I'd ask you to consider the following three changes in your present approach.

Add Loft to the Driver to Give Lift to Your Drives. My present driver is a little straighter-faced than normal at about nine degrees. The average driver has a club face that slants at an angle of eleven degrees —which isn't very much loft in terms of getting the ball airborne. For most golfers, the effect of looking down at such steep-faced clubs is worrisome. It makes you want to try harder to manipulate the ball up into the air, because you unconsciously believe the club itself isn't suited to do the job. Trouble is, if you believe the club can't do the job. it won't.

Psychologically and in terms of overall swing rhythm, most golfers would be better off using a driver with more than the average amount of loft built into the face. I used to drive with a one-and-a-half wood myself. A two wood or even a three wood will get you swinging more smoothly from off the tee, the ball will take flight more readily, and the comparatively few yards you may lose on the drive will be compensated for by greater consistency.

Pick a Target Area You Can Reach. It's unrealistic to expect every tee shot to cover the distance you achieved with the biggest tee shot of your career. Play to an area that you *know* you can reach comfortably and chances are you will pass it, because you'll swing more freely and generate more club-head speed. But try to reach that faraway spot and you'll tense up and overswing. Not only will you fall short of your target, but you'll often miss the fairway altogether.

Aim for the Fat Side of the Fairway. Even if a hole is dead straight, there's usually something out there—a bunker, a water hazard, trees, or such—that makes getting to the green at least slightly easier coming in from one side of the fairway than from the other. Your job is to observe the way the hole is designed and then hit toward the side of the fairway that would leave you sitting pretty for the shot.

Playing for an area to the right or to the left of the center of the fairway accomplishes two things. First, it removes the pressure to produce that next-to-impossible "straight shot" that aiming dead center would otherwise tend to create. Second, it focuses your attention and gets you into a mood of higher concentration for the shot.

Caution: You should always pick a generous patch of fairway as your target for a tee shot. Save more precise targeting for later in the hole—when you're trying to hit the flag with your short swing. Obviously it is important for a tee shot to be accurate, in that it should land in the fairway, and preferably in an area from which you can hit unobstructedly on your second shot. What I'm really saying here is that it is unrealistic to expect a tee shot to be *precise*. Aiming at a dime with the driver just isn't reasonable, and if it isn't reasonable your mind isn't really going to buy it, which is bound to add tension and confusion to your efforts.

When you learn to look down the fairway from each tee with your second shot in mind, you're beginning to think smart on the golf course. For some years, early in my career, I didn't have the sense to apply this bit of logic to my own game. I won a fair number of tournaments in those days, but I daresay I would have won a whole lot more if I had played for position on more of my drives and stopped going for the wild blue yonder every time I teed it up.

Of course, the big tee shot was considered the main attraction in my game for the galleries. Tournament organizers would pair me with other long-ball hitters every chance they got. I'd find myself reaching to the bottoms of my shoes to outdrive sluggers like Jimmy Thompson, or trying to reach every par-5 in two. Naturally I paid dearly for this extra power when my all-out shots strayed—as they often did—into trees or ponds.

As it turned out, once I throttled down and swung more for position than length, I began to play better than ever—I was leading money winner and Vardon Trophy winner (for lowest overall stroke average) for two years running after I made the change.

AVOID THE SECOND-SHOT SLUMP

Many golfers seem to experience a kind of mental lapse after driving into good position on the fairway. Their minds jump ahead to what's going to take place on the green—to their chances of making par or birdie. Or, in the space of time it takes to get to their ball, their minds stray to something else altogether . . . the conversation in the foursome . . . a duck flying by . . . last night's dinner. This kind of breakdown in concentration is, in my view, responsible for 90 percent of the mistakes made in golf between tee and green.

Two good ways to sustain your concentration on the way to the ball are to remind yourself of the type of swing you must execute for the second shot, and to figure out the club you should use.

First, remind yourself of the nature of the fairway swing you will be making next, and how it differs from the full swing you made on the tee, in that you will be endeavoring to deliver a slightly more downward

149

blow while relying on the loft of the club to get the ball airborne. Remind yourself particularly that the club is built to do that job, provided you swing correctly.

Second, begin the process of determining the yardage and selecting the club you need to cover that yardage. Even before you've reached the exact position of your second shot, you can roughly estimate that your next shot calls for "anywhere from a four iron to a six iron," say, or "an eight iron or seven iron." That way, by the time you do reach the ball, you'll have narrowed down your choice effectively—and, more important, kept your mind focused on the job at hand. When you reach the ball, you'll be able to pick the exact club quickly, and thus minimize any tendency to become nervous or tense by mulling over the shot.

It won't take long for you to make your final choice of club if you know how to judge distance. Determining the "yards to go" requires a certain amount of guesswork, sometimes even when you're on a course that is familiar to you, for it is the nature of the game to be playing from unfamiliar locations at least a few times every round—and in the case of the hacker, many more times than a few.

The only way for most golfers to get a feeling for yardage is to step off shots consciously, in order to get to know their own distances with each club. Once you've gone through that kind of experience, it is easier to compute distance by thinking, "It looks like a seven iron," than by thinking, "It looks like 150 yards, therefore a seven iron." In other words, it's easier to correlate distance to an experience you've actually had than to bare numbers. But that does not insure you from being misled by such factors as water, which tends to make a shot look longer than it is, or by dips and rises in the terrain, which can also disguise yardage. On a golf course you play regularly, actual yardages can be established from key points in the fairway through experience. On strange courses, you must rely more on your own judgment and the standard distance markers than have come into common use these days.

Many golfers are constantly guilty of wishful thinking about their own strengths, and thus consistently underclub their second shots. A fellow says to himself, "Hell, I can get home with a four wood," when in fact he could no more get there with a four wood than he could kill a bear with a B.B. gun. Don't count on giving every shot your Sunday punch. Take one more club than you think you need and you'll start finishing at or above the pin, instead of in the trap or lake fronting the green most of the time.

COPING WITH UNUSUAL LIES

A large part of the problem of handling the second shot on every hole (except par-3 holes where, hopefully, your second shot will be a putt) is coping with nonlevel lies. You seldom get a perfectly even stance for your second shot, as you always do for your opening shot, and your adjustment to this variable must be consciously and carefully made.

Uneven lies require (1) that you redeploy your weight to ensure good balance, and (2) that you make any adjustments in your grip position and ball position needed to ensure meeting the ball at the bottom of your swing arc. Your normal turn and swing arc should *not* change in any way, although this is the first thing most hackers instinctively do when faced with an uneven lie.

Downhill Lie. In playing from a downhill lie, you should first select a club that will compensate for the tendency of the ball to follow the slope of the ground and thus to fly lower than normal. If the distance to your target calls for a seven iron, you should play an eight iron instead. The added loft of the eight iron will compensate for the tendency of the ball to fly low, and produce what is in effect your normal seven iron shot.

In assuming your stance, line up so that you are aiming slightly to the *left* of the target. You do that because, in swinging down and through the ball in a downhill lie, you are almost certain to impart a little slice spin to the shot. Aiming left compensates for the slice.

Also, in assuming your stance, position the ball so it is slightly back of center. You should do this because the low point of the swing arc will naturally occur earlier than when you are playing from a level lie.

The point of these adjustments, remember, is to permit you to execute your *normal* swing. You defeat the purpose of the adjustments if you attempt to change your swing in any way—in an effort to scoop the ball up, for instance.

Uphill Lie. In playing a shot from an uphill lie, you must again select a club the loft of which will compensate for the tendency of the ball to follow the slope of the ground and thus fly higher than normal. Consequently, if the distance to your target calls for a seven iron, the actual club to be played is a six iron, in that it will make the ball fly lower and thereby produce what is, in effect, your normal seven iron shot.

In assuming your stance, line up so that you are aiming slightly to the *right* of the target. In swinging down and through the ball on an uphill lie, you will impart a certain amount of hook spin to the shot. Aiming right compensates for that.

On an uphill lie your weight will tend to be primarily on the rear foot, which is bad because it encourages you to fall away from the shot during the actual swing. To prevent this, bend your left knee more than usual, so that more weight gathers on the left side and balance is restored. (Note that the downhill lie tends to put most of the weight on the left side, but that, since this is where it should be at impact, it does not need to be redistributed.)

The low point of the swing arc tends to be moved forward when playing from an uphill lie, so position the ball off the inside of the left heel and you'll make contact with it at the right time and place.

Sidehill Lies. Sidehill lies in which the ball is either below or above your feet in the stance—require fewer adjustments but are actually a bit harder to play than uphill or downhill lies. Gravity tends to want to disrupt your swing, and you must be especially conscious of keeping your balance.

When the ball is lower than your feet, extend your effective shaft length by gripping as far up on the club handle as you can while still maintaining full control over the club. That will add a bit more comfortable "reach" to your address. You will feel a tendency to fall into the shot, so bend your knees a little more than normal to make sure your weight is firmly settled on your heels; that way you won't fall off balance when you swing.

When the ball is higher than your feet, simply choke down on the club handle and make sure your weight is centered on the *balls* of your feet.

Rough. In playing from rough, concentrate on swinging with a feeling of extra firmness in your arms and hands to prevent the tall grass from slowing down or twisting the club head before it meets the ball.

In especially heavy rough, don't try to obtain vast distance on your escape, but instead concentrate on getting the ball up and out, and back into play on the fairway.

Use a well-lofted club to make sure the initial trajectory of the shot has enough height to clear the rough. If you use a seven iron or longer club, I suggest you open the clubface slightly to increase its effective loft.

Never use a wood club from the rough unless the ball is lying decently, and then never use it unless you absolutely require the extra distance. Chances are you'll always be better off playing a lofted iron any time you leave the close-mown surface.

Over and Under Obstacles. Occasionally you'll find yourself behind a tree or other obstacle, from which escape is only possible via an extra-high shot over the obstacle, or an unusually low-flying shot that will pass under it safely.

To put extra height on a shot, play it more forward in your stance than you normally would for the club selected. That will increase the effective loft on the club. Then concentrate on striking down on the ball rather than trying to "help" it up, which is the temptation in these circumstances, with fat or scooped shots the usual result.

To hit a lower-than-normal shot requires playing the ball farther back in your stance, and also a little farther away from your body. That way you'll swing at the ball on a flatter plane and make contact when the club face is partly closed, ensuring a lower trajectory.

Remember, your main goal in playing from any unusual lie is to set you and your club up to the ball in such a way that the flight of the ball changes without your basic swing changing. If you can absorb the knowledge required to know how to set yourself up to the ball with confidence in all these situations, and without tampering with your swing, you'll become a much more effective player between tee and green.

15: Sharpening Your Short Game

THE area within a hundred yards of the green on each hole is where most handicap golfers could dramatically improve their scoring ability, by learning and practicing the basic techniques of pitching, chipping, and sand play. This is where you can make up for a lot of weaknesses in your long game. I've seen golfers who can only drive the ball 150 yards shoot in the low 80s, thanks to a good short game.

Generally speaking, these techniques belong in the category of the "short swing," which I described earlier. For the pitch, chip, and sand shot, your weight must remain firmly on your left side throughout the stroke, primarily because the reduced shaft length shortens the swing arc to such a degree that it is all but impossible to make a well-timed weight shift. Remember, too, that the only reason for shifting your weight is to put extra power into the shot, and for these short shots near the green extra power just isn't required.

The first rule in pitching, chipping, and sand play is to keep your head extremely still. The slightest sway in the swing's axis on these precision shots throws the downswing off line and ruins the shot.

You need to place special emphasis on a steady head because there is a tendency to become slack in the upper body on all short shots. I think this happens because the solid anchoring of the lower body onto the left side gives the golfer a false sense of confidence in his overall posture, as a result of which his upper body position gets raggedy.

Keeping the weight to the left and maintaining a very steady head are integral to all short shots. Individually, the pitch, chip, and sand shot make certain special additional demands, which I'll now briefly describe.

THE PITCH SHOT

In my opinion the pitching wedge is the third most important club in the bag—after the putter and the driver. With a little practice it can help most handicap golfers improve their scoring dramatically. From within a hundred yards you can put the ball inside one-putt range with the pitching wedge more often than with any other club, mainly because of the extra control made available through the heavy spin this club imparts to the ball.

The pitch is played with an open stance—you're facing the target more, to see it better. And it's played with your feet close together—at half the distance of the width of your normal stance—to discourage swaying. Position the ball in the center of your stance to make sure your club face makes contact with it before it reaches the bottom of its comparatively steep arc. The downward blow must be emphasized here because of the tendency to try to "scoop" the ball with your hands on these short shots.

The backswing on the pitch ranges in length from one-half to three-quarters of a normal backswing. All that is needed is to get the club far enough back into position to strike the ball with a crisp, downward accelerating blow—the club will take care of the rest.

On short pitches—such as when you're trying to drop the ball on the green just beyond a sand trap—it's a good idea to choke down on the club handle. That will increase your "feel" for the stroke at the same time as it shortens your backswing, and thus keep you from hitting the shot too far.

THE CHIP SHOT

Like the pitch shot, you play the chip shot from an open stance, with your weight firmly on your left side and your head positioned over the ball and kept very steady. Unlike the pitch shot, the chip shot is made with no wrist action whatsoever. A firm left hand and lack of wrist break will keep the backswing nice and short, from where the ball will be struck crisply, with the hands leading the club head firmly through impact.

Think of the chip shot as being a precise stroke with a minimum of moving parts—like the putting stroke, almost. The length of the backswing and the firmness with which the stroke is made determine distance, but neither swing length nor swing firmness can be computed to the point where the golfer can effectively control the shot by trying to "calibrate" his backswing or firmness. Just as on putts, the golfer must rely on his sense of distance and touch in chipping the ball. These are capabilities that can only be developed through practice and experience. Practice plus experience eventually lead to usable instinct.

You can chip with practically any iron—many tour players are deadly chippers using pitching wedges or sand irons. But the club I recommend to most average golfers for chipping is the seven iron. It has enough loft to get the ball sufficiently in the air to drop it on the green, yet will also produce a lot of roll, which is easier to judge than flight for most players.

The pitch shot and the chip shot should both be treated as highly individual control strokes, in which your personal judgment and touch must ultimately dictate the length and force of the stroke. Gripping down on the club handle and shortening the backswing are matters of guesswork at first, but of instinct once you've had a little practice at it. For both types of shots, it is better to get a clear mental picture of the distance that has to be covered by the shot, and then rely on instinct, rather than thinking over-mechanically, for example, of precisely how far back to take the club.

SAND SHOTS

Learning to play from sand not only saves you several strokes a round, but enables you to go for the green with a far more positive attitude on all your approach shots. Golfers with no faith in their sand game are frequently forced by their dread of bunkers into tense swinging and steering on the majority of approach shots.

For the basic explosion shot, play the ball well forward in your stance, about opposite your left heel. This ensures that you'll get enough height on the shot to clear the bunker wall. Open your stance a little to get a better look at your target and also to encourage the more upright backswing that, again, will help you to get the ball up high, and that also is a big factor in having the ball land softly and settle quickly on the green.

In taking your stance, it is vital to wiggle into a firm footing with both feet, to prevent yourself from spinning out during the swing. Get your weight on the left side and keep it there just as on any short shot.

Slightly open the face of the club—I am assuming it is a proper sand wedge—to make it easier for the club to slice cleanly through the sand underneath the ball. Think of the movement of the club through the sand as a kind of knifing action. Aim to slice the club head into the sand at a point about two inches behind the ball *and keep that club head going at all times*. Most balls left in traps remain there because the golfer quit on the shot.

Think of yourself taking your normal short shot swing when playing from sand. Actually, you will swing more upright, because of your open stance, but don't strive for a significantly different swing or you will likely force the shot—a fatal tendency in sand.

On the backswing, keep your left hand firm and your head over the ball. Pull down on the club with the last two fingers of your left hand to start the downswing, then keep on pulling with the left hand to create the slicing action of the club head through the sand beneath the ball.

The depth of the cut you take in sand with your club will vary with the type of sand used in the bunkers. If it is light, airy sand, the "divot" will be fairly shallow. If the sand is wet or particularly firm, the divot should be deeper. For a deeper divot, hit down and under the ball a little more firmly than you normally would. But be sure always to keep that club head going into a full follow-through.

With a strong, short game, a golfer can pitch, chip, and scramble to a score of his choosing, just about. But because the short game requires so much touch and feel and finesse, it's the toughest part of golf in which to become expert and to sustain in peak condition. It takes a lot of thought and practice and experience. Remember that, after a layoff, your short game will always take longer to get back into good running condition than your long shots. And the only way to get it back is through practice.

16: "Sidesaddle" Putting Can Work for You, Too

I consider my present sidesaddle putting style a *conservative* approach to putting, and in that sense I believe it carries an important message for most golfers, young or old. Namely, "Avoid three-putt greens at all costs." If you can figure out a way to do that, you are bound to score better very quickly.

My sidesaddle putting style is the main reason I've been able to stay in contention in the tournaments I enter every year. As of this writing, I'm averaging about thirty-three putts a round in tournament play. That, combined with hitting the fairways and greens pretty regularly, gives me scores close to par or better most of the time. Before I changed to my nerve-free method, I was starting to take forty-one or forty-two putts per round on the average. I had no chance at all to win even bus fare that way.

The yips got to me almost ten years ago. I'd always considered myself a pretty good putter, especially on the long putts. Then my nerves started acting up. Putting in my conventional style, I'd push one, pull one, hit them everywhere but in the hole.

I knew I had to find a different way to get the ball in the hole; I was too thirsty for competition just to quit. So at first I tried putting croquet style, straddling the line of the putt and swinging the putter between my legs. I started using this style quite suddenly, during the 1966 PGA Championship at Firestone. I was leading the tournament in the third round, but on the tenth green my hand twitched in the middle of my putting stroke and I hit the ball twice. I knew right then I had to do something about my nerves, so beginning on the next hole I started putting croquet style, straddling the line of the putt and swinging the putter between my legs. Well, I made three putts in a row, and Don January, my playing partner, said, "Hell, why don't you putt like that all the time?"

That's exactly what I did, at least until the U.S. Golf Association outlawed the croquet style (technically, the USGA outlawed "straddling the line" when putting).

In the meantime, I'd built up a certain amount of skill in the new style. Actually, I'd been aware of the croquet putting style ever since caddying as a ten-year-old for an old-timer who used that method with a homemade T-shaped putter, and who had gotten around the greens pretty well with it. And later I'd often played lawn croquet here and in England and done pretty well at it. I'd even tried the style in tournaments on an occasional basis, just for fun, long before I really had call to.

So I had confidence in the method, and was getting proficient at it when the USGA ruled it out. I think the blue-blazer squad was disturbed to see the croquet style catching on at golf clubs after I had introduced it on tour. Anyway, I checked the new rule when it was announced, and then literally sidestepped it. That is, I moved my right foot over to join my left foot in my putting stance (so that I was no longer straddling the line), threw my hips out to one side, and bent over with my putter, just as I had when putting croquet style. And that's how my sidesaddle putting style was started.

As in the croquet style, I use only the big muscles of the right arm and shoulder in the sidesaddle style, taking the little muscles of the hand and wrist completely out. I recommend the style especially to older golfers who are starting to have trouble with their nerves on the greens —especially on those murderous little putts.

And don't hesitate to try the style (which I describe in detail at the end of this chapter) just because it looks different. One year at the annual Masters Champions' dinner, Bobby Jones turned to me, frowned, and said, "You know, Sam, that's a hell of a way to putt."

"Well, Bob," I replied, "when you come in off the course they don't ask you how. They ask how many."

Today that is still a valid defense for sidesaddle, or any other legitimate putting style you happen to be able to use effectively, no matter what it looks like to others. If you're embarrassed, take comfort in the fact that the galleries laughed and snickered when I first started experimenting with a putting style that would save me from the yips—or what the English call, more accurately, the twitches. The galleries don't snicker any more.

Sidesaddle happens to highlight a couple of putting fundamentals that are important to all golfers, and not just "twitchy" seniors. The two most important characteristics of the style are: (1) it keeps the wrists out of the putting stroke; (2) it gets the first putt close enough to the hole to make the second putt a "gimme."

The best putters on tour today use little or no wrist action in their strokes. This is a change from earlier days on tour. I myself was strictly a wrist putter when I first went on tour. I had developed a very soft touch from putting the lightning-fast greens at the Homestead where I played as a kid, and that's really why I started winning tournaments so quickly after turning pro. Today's youngsters are coming on tour with far less wristy strokes.

The big money riding on short putts today makes the pros vulnerable to the yips long before their time. And it is now well established that putting with some kind of arm-and-shoulder method protects you from nervous tension far better than any method stressing wrist action. So, if you're using your wrists in your putting stroke to any degree, bear in mind that you're opening yourself up to a rash of three-putt greens.

The other big plus in the sidesaddle style—and something that should figure in the game of all golfers, no matter what their putting method— is its emphasis on getting that first putt within makable distance. Just as your main goal on the first stroke you take on any hole—the tee shot—is to hit the ball where you can find it, your main goal on the first stroke you take on any green is to putt the ball where you can make the next one. Lagging successfully to the area of the hole, rather than putting right at the hole and risking running well past it, should be your standard strategy on long putts.

That approach is conservative in the sense that you don't feel yourself boldly charging that cup as though you owned it. But it's also conservative in the sense that it may *conserve* you the extra stroke it would take to get the ball into the hole after that first bold putt rolls way past.

I think it is advisable to try generally to sink putts that are within about twenty feet of the hole, no matter what your putting method. (I'm talking here about ordinary golfers now, and not the pros, some of whom have the confidence and the proven technique to try to sink putts from sixty feet or more). But putts any longer than twenty feet should be lagged to within a two-foot range of the hole—at least by the handicap player. The golfer who tries to hole all his putts is usually the one with the most three-putt greens.

Get the wrist out of your stroke and get the three-putt greens out of your score—those are my general guidelines for all golfers. More specifically, but again regardless of the particular putting method preferred, I think more golfers would be better putters if (1) they followed a set routine, or S.O.P. (just like our S.O.P. for shot making), in approaching and making a putt; and (2) they learned to gauge the backswing to a feeling for the *speed* required for the putt, rather than its line.

Too many golfers, especially in this day of anxiety about slow play, rush their putting preparation. Provided you step on the green with a specific S.O.P., I think you can learn to putt without wasting time, but at the same time without losing the opportunity to make the putt, which only a very deliberate and concentrated approach can provide for you.

Finding the path or line you want your putt to travel across the green requires checking the approach from directly across the cup and from one side of the cup. That way you'll see clearly the actual contours of the green, which are always a determinant of the speed at which the ball rolls, and you'll be able to establish whether the grass is growing away from or toward the hole. If the grass is growing towards you, the grass will appear darker and the putt will require more firmness. If the grass is growing away from you, the grass will appear glossier or shinier and the putt will tend to roll faster.

In judging slope, you must establish the angle, if any, of the green overall. If the entire green is built on a tilted axis, your putt will tend to fall in the direction of the low point, regardless of the slope in the putting area—putts always tend to run toward any nearby water hazards, for example. Then you must establish the slope—again, if any—of the green between the area of your ball and the area of the cup.

Once you have a general feeling for slope, and have also noted whether the grain is fast or slow, you're ready to check your line for a final time from directly behind the ball, before stepping up to make the putt. The investigation so far has served one more important purpose—by walking the distance from the cup back to your ball you have acquired a physical sense of the distance of the putt, which will be critical in choosing the speed at which to strike the putt.

Once you've placed your putter behind the ball, square to the starting line on which you want the ball to travel, you're ready to remove all considerations about line from your mind and to concentrate solely on striking the ball so it carries to the cup—or, in the case of the lag putt, to within a two-foot circle of the cup.

Don't stand over the putt at this point, or you'll become beset by doubt and confusion and fear. And never second-guess the line you've selected. Concentrate solely on the speed you want the putt to travel and on hitting the ball squarely on the sweet spot of your putter blade. That concentration will automatically produce the length of backswing the putt requires. If you think about backswing length consciously, your stroke will rarely be fluid. The analogous situation occurs in any shot: when you think about something in your swing, instead of the timing you desire to impart to the swing overall, you tend to disrupt the mechanics of the swing.

HOW TO PUTT SIDESADDLE

The Putter. Center-shafted putters work better in the sidesaddle method than blade putters or mallet-type putters, which have the shaft at the end of the blade. Whatever putter you select, however, I would suggest that you modify it in two ways.

1. Add a few inches of length to the grip handle so you won't have to bend over so far in setting up for the stroke.

2. Extend the grip down the shaft to a point midway between the original grip and the putter head. That will give you a more stable and consistent hold with your right hand in using the hands-apart grip that is essential for sidesaddle putting.

Your club professional can fix up your putter at small cost.

Grip. Treat the grip handle kind of like the squeeze stick in the cockpit of an airplane. Let your left thumb ride on the butt end of the grip and wrap the fingers of the left hand around the handle. In gripping the shaft of the putter with your right hand, let it run between the thumb and heel pads to the base of the forefinger. Then let the thumb

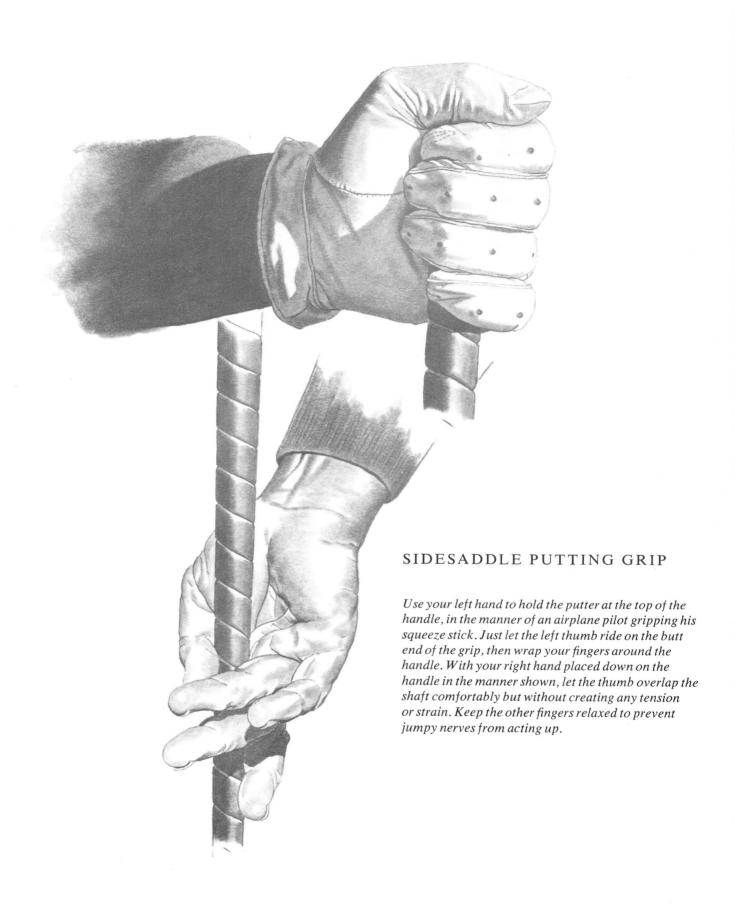

SIDESADDLE PUTTING GRIP

Use your left hand to hold the putter at the top of the
handle, in the manner of an airplane pilot gripping his
squeeze stick. Just let the left thumb ride on the butt
end of the grip, then wrap your fingers around the
handle. With your right hand placed down on the
handle in the manner shown, let the thumb overlap the
shaft comfortably but without creating any tension
or strain. Keep the other fingers relaxed to prevent
jumpy nerves from acting up.

SIDESADDLE PUTTING STANCE

The idea is to stand in a comfortable, balanced position at a slight angle to the target line to give your arm a bit more room to operate on the backswing. Also, make sure that you play the ball far enough off your right foot to avoid hitting your foot with the putter on the backswing. You can sight down the line to the cup with both eyes, which is actually an advantage that sidesaddle has over conventional putting styles.

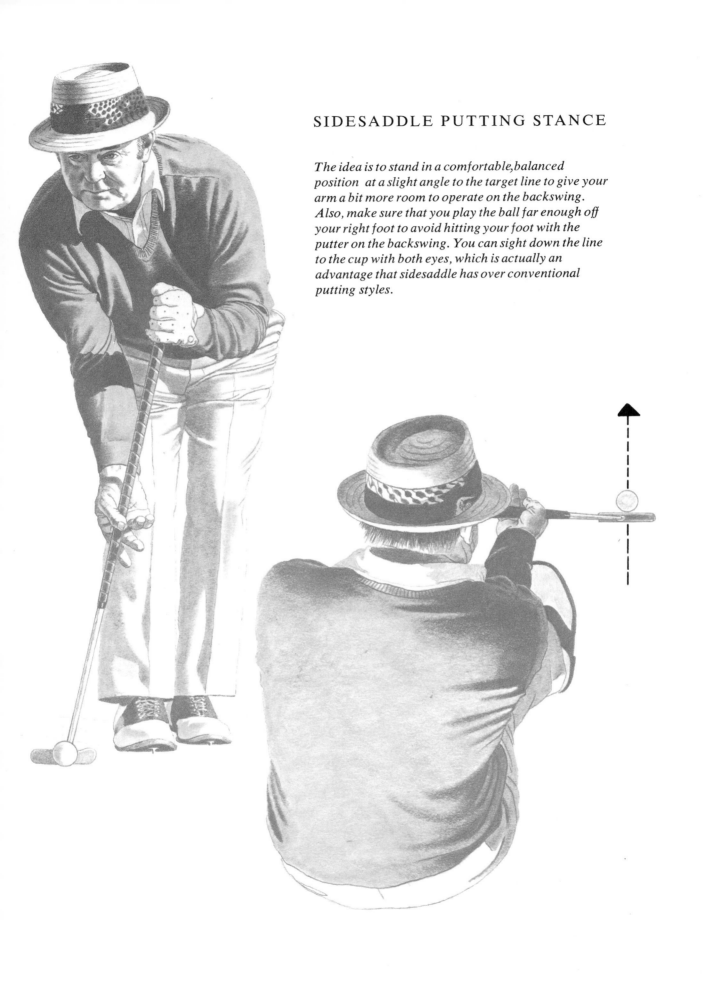

SIDESADDLE PUTTING STROKE

The sidesaddle putting stroke is made entirely with the right arm and shoulder. Make sure your right hand and wrist remain completely inactive or the pendulum motion will be disrupted. The left hand serves as a hinge for the stroking action and it, too, should be kept from jumping into the act. The overall motion is akin to that of rolling a ball underhanded along the ground. Extra care must be taken to hit the ball squarely with the putter head, especially on long putts. The big danger in sidesaddle is topping the ball.

overlap the shaft comfortably, but don't crook it around with any tension. The idea is to keep those jumpy nerves in fingers and wrists out of positions of influence.

The Stance. Stand up to the side of the ball with your feet close together for balance and pointing a little to the left of your target line, to create a bit more clearance for your arm swing. Bend your knees slightly so you can lean over comfortably from the waist. Your right arm should hang straight but not stiff, and your left elbow should be tucked in close to your side.

Play the ball far enough off the right foot so that you don't risk hitting your foot with the putter by mistake when it goes back. You should have the feeling that your head is over the target line and that you're looking straight down the line to the cup with both eyes. Actually, in this way you'll find you are able to sight your putts better than with the conventional style.

I play the ball from three to five inches ahead of my right foot—toward the hole—depending on the length of the putt. Determine your own natural ball positioning by discovering where you can most comfortably strike the ball at the bottom of the stroke.

The Stroke. Stroke the ball firmly, *using your right arm and right shoulder only*. Make sure you keep your wrist inactive, that there's no hinging or unhinging whatsoever in the stroke. Also, don't grab or clasp the shaft with your right hand during the stroke or you'll lose all smoothness.

The right arm swings like a pendulum in the stroke. The left arm remains still, the upper arm close to the body, the forearm pointing at the target. The grip of the left hand acts as the hinge on which the putter swings. It takes no active part in the stroke except on long putts of forty feet or more. On such long putts the left hand can be used to help lever the putter head through the ball more firmly.

There's a tendency, using the sidesaddle method, to come up short on all putts simply because only one hand is actively involved in the stroke. Experience will teach you the right amount of stroke to use on shorter putts to get the ball to the hole. On longer putts, it's helpful also to use the left hand to pull back on the club handle as the right hand pushes the putter head forward.

As in any style of putting, the degree of backswing you need depends entirely on your feeling for the putt itself. First, concentrate on hitting the ball squarely in back on all putts and making sure it rolls across the green without any jerks or jumps. Then you can start connecting your feeling for the speed of the putt with the amount of backswing you use.

The sidesaddle putting stroke has the same feeling to it as does rolling a ball smoothly underhanded. If you're having trouble getting the stroke to work smoothly, assume your stance without the putter and practice rolling the ball to the cup a few times. Then try it with the putter again.

Most golfers plagued by the putting yips could benefit almost immediately by using the sidesaddle style. It takes just a little bit of practice to overcome the awkward feeling in the setup; it also takes a certain amount of individualizing. How much length you add to your putter grip is strictly a personal matter. To a slightly lesser extent, so are the questions of ball position in the stance and alignment of the body. Actually, it's likely that sidesaddle lends itself to as many variations as conventional putting does.

Extremely long putts—putts in the seventy- to eighty-foot range—require special care using the sidesaddle method because there's a danger of either leaving the putts well short or half topping them. A little extra practice will help to develop the solid contact needed.

Medium length putts—putts in the thirty- to forty-foot range—are easy to handle relatively quickly putting sidesaddle. Most golfers should be able to start lagging these putts to the hole successfully after only half an hour's practice with the style.

Short putts—ten- to fifteen-footers—take a lot of practice, no matter how you putt.

171

That short range of putt is the area in which I've been weakest since going to the sidesaddle style. The reason is simple: I haven't had the urge to practice those putts enough. After age sixty, long training sessions somehow begin to lose their appeal. If I did practice those ten-footers more, I might be able to really put the heat on those kids out there on tour.

17: Four Attitudes You Need to Win

EARLIER in this book I outlined what I considered to be the main physical traits of the good golfer. In this concluding chapter I want to describe the mental and emotional traits that I feel should be nurtured by any person who wants to compete at golf well and long.

I hope it's obvious to every reader that such acts as throwing clubs in anger, or quitting on a hole in disgust, disrupt the mind and body and ruin the golfing mood. But rather than list such obvious emotional excesses to avoid, I'd like to suggest four larger attitudes for golfers to try to grow into—especially those golfers who already *do* throw clubs or quit on holes. They are the attitudes of *confidence, concentration, detachment,* and *desire*.

Even if it were possible, I would not recommend that you try to overhaul your basic personality in order to play better golf. That would be as fruitless as trying to get you to change your natural swing tempo, or to eliminate an ingrained personal mannerism from your swing.

However, if you can foster these four attitudes within the limits set by your personality, you'll be able to make use of your knowledge and ability with less interference from your worst impulses. And that means fewer missed shots and tactical blunders, and more winning scores.

CONFIDENCE

When you think you can make a shot, you usually come pretty close to doing so. When you don't think you can, you generally miss by a mile. That pretty much sums up how important confidence is in the game of golf.

The only way to build *realistic* confidence in yourself is through practice. As I've told thousands of weekend golfers over the years, golf technique is not picked up down at the corner store. It is acquired through long and hard labor on the practice tee. That is the only way you can build faith in your ability and trust in your equipment.

I've always tried not to have a "worst" shot—a shot I hated to face. If I was having trouble with one part of my game, such as my long irons or my sand play, I would go out and practice until the problem was removed. I've also made it a point never to *avoid* using certain clubs, as so many golfers do, because of fear of not being able to handle them. If my seven iron was giving me trouble, I would work with it until it produced the shots I desired—or get a new seven iron.

I think facing such problems head on and overcoming them is the only way to sustain confidence in yourself as a golfer over the long haul. Take inventory of your game after every day of play, as I do, then pick out what has to be improved and go to work on it.

An aid to confidence is staying in good physical shape. A tired body will affect your thinking and your tempo—especially on the back nine. If you feel good about yourself physically, you're always likely to perform better on the golf course.

Basically, though, confidence grows out of nailing down your technique through practice. When you trust your technique, you hold the club lightly and swing positively and well within yourself.

CONCENTRATION

Most ordinary golfers don't have an attention span at the ball that is either long enough or intense enough. You must concentrate intensely, if for only a few seconds, before each shot, but it must be *total concentration,* or your technique will never work smoothly.

Think about strategy and shot-making technique throughout the round where and when you feel it is called for. *But when you are standing over the shot, put everything out of your mind except one key technical thought and a definite mental impression or "feel" for the timing the shot requires.*

A few seconds of concentration is all the mental effort a golf shot demands, but it must be *intense.*

Concentrate, but don't "imaginate." I picture the flight I want my ball to take before I make my shot, but then I pay attention to what I'm doing with the club, not to where the ball is going. Too much concern with the target risks bringing in worries about going left or right, or puts traps or water or other hazards into your head. Or you might start thinking about how you botched the same shot last week. Think about the swing that will get the ball to the target once you've decided on how the ball must perform to reach it.

Good concentration on the shot itself allows you to swing with the changing conditions that the game always imposes on every golfer. If your mind focuses on the bad weather or the odd lie rather than on the shot you're about to make, you won't swing in your groove. Concentration allows you to burn through those mental fogs and play the stroke sharply.

DETACHMENT

Golf can build up more animosities in a man than any other game I know. A player feels on top of the world on one hole and ready for murder on the next, all because of one missed putt, or an unlucky lie, or a demoralizingly good shot by an opponent.

To be consistently effective, you must put a certain distance between yourself and what happens to you out on the golf course. I'm not suggesting you can be *indifferent* to results: you must *care intensely* in order to score well in golf. But you also must protect yourself from the consequences when things don't go as planned. That I call "detachment."

There are two simple ways to improve your own detachment on the course.

1. Find an overall playing pace that's right for you, and then stick to that pace whenever you play, no matter who hits where, and no matter how fast or slowly your playing partners want to get through the round. My old South African friend Bobby Locke was an absolute master of this, and so is Jack Nicklaus today. Choose a pace that will keep your adrenaline flowing in just the right amount, and that, as it becomes habitual to you, will tend to keep you on the same emotional track when things go either very well or very poorly.

2. Try very hard never to follow one bad shot with another. So many golfers ruin a hole, and eventually an entire round, by letting one bad shot totally disrupt their rhythm and their concentration. Understand that even touring pros shooting in the 60s always wish they could replay at least half a dozen shots of the round. If you can school yourself to get over a bad shot *immediately after it's happened,* you'll scatter your inevitable mis-hits through a round and your total score will be much lower.

DESIRE

Desire is vitally important in golf because there is always the challenge of change and adaptation to overcome in order to compete well at the game.

Various matches and opponents, different courses and playing conditions, odd lies of all kinds, and the endless variables in the swing and in the art of scoring—all make the challenge of golf extremely complex. Thus a deep and abiding rather than a casual commitment is required in order to meet the total challenge. Of course, that is also what gives the game such endless fascination.

In recent years my own desire to compete has been sufficiently strong to help me completely change my putting stroke, as I've already described in detail, and also to alter my basic long-shot pattern from a draw to a fade. Both changes were concessions to age, of a sort. I started putting differently because of jumpy nerves in my hands and wrists. I began to fade the ball because of tendonitis in my left arm—I've had to hit more with my right hand in the full swing because my left arm won't stay straight under the strain of the downswing.

The point is not that I have succeeded in overcoming the infirmities of age, however. The point is rather that the natural decline in nervous composure and muscular strength, as one grows older, should be treated as a factor demanding adaptation—another bad lie or tricky opponent —rather than as a reason to give up. I believe that is why golf really is a game for a lifetime. It's probably the only sport that *you* have to give up, rather than its forcing you out.

Many older players become disconsolate when they realize they are hitting shorter and shorter off the tee and yipping more and more putts on the greens. It's my belief there's always a way to continue if your desire is strong enough: for example, such players could minimize their loss in power by using softer-shafted clubs, and they certainly might benefit on the greens by experimenting with potentially more stable putting styles, as I did.

But instead—like untutored hackers—most attempt to solve their problems *without changing anything*. That, of course, makes them even more unhappy, and before long they take the fatal step—they start to play less frequently, and soon lose so much touch with the game that eventually they give it up completely.

I would not be competing effectively on tour in my sixties if it were not for the fact that I have always played golf regularly, rarely missing a week without some play or practice. Handicap golfers need not play as much as I do, nor have anything like my competitive goals, but certainly all golfers who do stay closely in touch with their games are better off in the long run.

The curious thing is that, yes, my strong desire to play has kept me going over the years, and has gotten me through some hard changes in my game. But the continuity in my play—my playing on a regular basis instead of throwing in the towel—seems to have kept up my *desire* to compete, which is as strong today as it has ever been.

You need desire to play golf—but you need to keep playing the game to maintain the desire. That's something worth thinking about, no matter how old you are, or what you shoot.